Knowledge that Counts in a Global Community

In the first decades of the new millennium, we are faced with increasing pressures relating to climate change and the sustainability of life on Earth. Concerned citizens are realizing that the responsibility to respond is both local and global. There is an increasing sense of urgency about the need to reform the processes of schooling and curriculum to better prepare students for global citizenship. Educators, policy makers and the wider community are seeking information about how to proceed with this reform effort, particularly how alternative and integrated approaches to curriculum can be used to engage students with the important issues of our time.

Knowledge that Counts in a Global Community explores the potential contribution of curriculum integration in a context where school curricula are typically segregated by discipline. It offers curriculum integration as a powerful tool for educating young citizens so that they can understand and respond to global concerns. It argues for an informed citizenry who can think broadly across disciplines, and contribute sensibly and pragmatically to local problems with an eye on how this translates to making a global difference. In its examination of the twin themes of global knowledge and curriculum integration, the book explores:

*   the nature of curriculum integration
*   the nature of knowledge
*   the nature of learning.

The authors reflect on these issues from perspectives gained by more than a decade of research in the area. Their in-depth, scholarly exploration and critical analysis of current approaches to curriculum introduces educators and academics to contemporary ways of conceptualizing the complexities of, and relationships among, curriculum integration, knowledge and learning. Throughout the book, the authors emphasize the central curriculum question: what kinds of outcomes do we want for students of the twenty-first century? This book provides a valuable resource for academic educators, researchers, teachers and others interested in educational policy reform.

Léonie Rennie is a Research Professor in the Office of Research and Development at Curtin University of Technology in Perth, Western Australia.

Grady Venville is a Professor in the Graduate School of Education at the University of Western Australia in Perth, Western Australia.

John Wallace is a Professor in the Ontario Institute for Studies in Education at the University of Toronto, Canada.

Knowledge that Counts in a Global Community

Exploring the contribution of integrated curriculum

Léonie Rennie,
Grady Venville and
John Wallace

Routledge
Taylor & Francis Group

LONDON AND NEW YORK

First published 2012
by Routledge
2 Park Square, Milton Park, Abingdon, Oxon OX14 4RN

Simultaneously published in the USA and Canada
by Routledge
711 Third Avenue, New York, NY 10017

Routledge is an imprint of the Taylor & Francis Group, an informa business

British Library Cataloguing in Publication Data
A catalogue record for this book is available from the British Library

Library of Congress Cataloging in Publication Data
Rennie, Léonie J.
Knowledge that counts in a global community: exploring the contribution
of the integrated curriculum/Léonie J. Rennie, Grady Venville, and
John Wallace.
    p. cm.
1. Interdisciplinary approach in education. 2. Education and globalization.
I. Venville, Grady Jane. II. Wallace, John (John William), 1947- III. Title.
LB2361.R45 2012
372.3—dc23   2011020907

ISBN: 978-0-415-57337-5 (hbk)
ISBN: 978-0-415-57338-2 (pbk)
ISBN: 978-0-203-81747-6 (ebk)

Typeset in Bembo
by Cenveo Publisher Services

Printed and bound in Great Britain by the MPG Books Group

CONTENTS

List of tables   vi
Preface   vii
Acknowledgements   xi

1   Mapping the territory: The background to curriculum
    integration   1

2   The nature of curriculum integration: Connection and
    approaches   16

3   Implementing curriculum integration: School and
    curriculum structures   35

4   Learning in integrated curriculum settings: Lenses,
    arguments and contexts   54

5   The status of school knowledge: Challenging the
    discipline-based structure   73

6   Knowledge that counts in a global community:
    Balance and connection   97

7   A new understanding of curriculum integration:
    Using a Worldly Perspective   116

Bibliography   121
Appendix: Description of case studies of integrated curriculum   130
Author index   137
Subject index   140

Tables

1.1 Summary of the research programme 8

2.1 Summary of case studies used as exemplars of approaches to curriculum integration 22

3.1 Summary of enabling and inhibiting conditions 38

3.2 A teaching framework incorporating a Worldly Perspective on curriculum integration 52

4.1 Class means and standard deviations for levels of agreement on statements about an integrated unit 66

6.1 Categories of ideas from students at Brampton High School about the question 'What do you know about midge?' 109

Preface

We are well into the twenty-first century. Early in the second decade of the new millennium, three of the stories dominating international media are the aftermath of the global financial crisis, the continuing tensions in the Middle East, and the generally accepted failure of the world's leaders to reach agreement for decisive action on climate change. More locally, we try to deal with human tragedies; the devastating earthquakes in several countries, for example, whose citizens immediately became reliant on the rest of the world to assist with medical aid, food and shelter. Diverse stories, but with a common thread. Ours is a connected world. No event or issue is isolated from every other. What happens anywhere in the world can effect each of us.

There are repercussions from this connectedness. On the one hand, rapid transport and fast international communications are melting away geographic boundaries. On the other hand, and despite mass human migration from troubled countries to others perceived to be less troubled, political, cultural and religious divides persist. Such problems have few boundaries, however. All of the world's people are threatened by the consequences of over-population, inadequacies in food production and distribution, and the continuing consumption of non-renewable resources. Our highly developed infrastructure, reliant on fast transport and electronic communication, leaves us vulnerable to cyber and other kinds of attack. Threats related to terrorism, strengthened in the last decade, persist and permeate our confidence in the future.

One might expect that the difficulties in dealing with an uncertain and unpredictable future are reflected in rapidly responding educational curricula designed to ready our children for the changing world outside of school. But this is not so. Readers concerned with education know that schools are very difficult to change. While the world is changing at an alarming pace, facilitated by a communications network that makes visible, in real time, what is happening on the other side of the world, students in schools sit mostly in desks in closed classrooms learning much the same language, history, mathematics and science that their parents learned a generation before. It is hard to see why students should perceive this kind of curriculum as the most relevant to their future needs, and most of them don't. Sadly, there is widespread disaffection with schooling today.

If schools are to fulfil their social role of preparing our youth to be responsible adults and sensible citizens in a world quite different from the one their
parents experienced after leaving school, the challenge is great indeed. There is
no lack of will. Teachers do not deliberately choose to implement curricula
they believe to be irrelevant and unhelpful to the future needs of their students.
They do their best in the circumstances in which they find themselves and
with the curriculum available to them. The problem is, what kind of curriculum is 'best'? What are the knowledge and skills that will prepare students for
an uncertain future? As is usual in questions of education, there is no single,
uniformly satisfying answer. This should not be surprising. Different students
in different classrooms in different countries have different circumstances and
different needs, and so there are innumerable solutions that have been, and are
being, proposed to address the problem. These attempted solutions are reflected
in the myriad curricula and sets of planned curricular outcomes that are put
forward and mandated to varying degrees by the authorities responsible for our
schools. What works best? What approaches to curriculum will prepare our
students most effectively for their diverse and uncertain futures?

This book is about some of these approaches. Our starting point is the
proposition that we live in a global community and we need to consider the
kind of knowledge that will help students find their way in their out-of-school
lives. We chose the term 'global community' carefully. Community conveys
a sense of fellowship, affinity, identity of character and joint ownership.
Although we still have to identify a single country of citizenship on our
passports, our community now is much broader than the country in which
we were born or now dwell. It is a global community, one that we share as
citizens with all others. We share its fellowship and camaraderie and, like it
or not, its connectedness means that we also have joint ownership of its
problems. Given this, and the requirement to prepare our youth to cope in this
global community, we need our schooling to provide them with 'knowledge
that counts'.

In particular, we explore in this book the contribution that can be made by
integrated curriculum to 'knowledge that counts'. Why have we chosen to
focus on integrated curriculum? Some years ago, we became intrigued by the
widespread interest in curricula described this way, seemingly regarded by
some as a panacea for the problems perceived about schooling, especially at
the level of middle school. Here, it was argued, significant changes occurred for
students as they moved from a primary school classroom, where they were
usually taught by one teacher, to a secondary school environment where they
were taught different subjects by different teachers in different classrooms.
At about the same time as these curricular and structural changes impacted the
student–teacher relationship, students were also experiencing the onset
of puberty, with different expectations for themselves as adolescents rather than
children. Together, these changes marked a stressful period of disaffection with
a kind of schooling perceived as irrelevant and potentially alienating. What was
it about an integrated curriculum that could ameliorate these problems and

connect students with the issues facing the global community? Popular books, such as those by Jacobs (1989), Fogarty (1991) and Drake (1993), and enthusiastic commentary by educators such as Beane (1991), were offset by notes of caution from others (e.g., Alleman and Brophy, 1993; Case, 1994). Clearly, integrated curriculum was not only a buzzword, even a slogan, of the 1980s and 1990s, but a disputed educational issue. What did it mean?

The word 'integrate' means to complete by the addition of parts or to combine parts into a whole. Thus 'integration' refers to the bringing together of parts. In the context of curriculum, the 'bringing together of parts' connotes 'curriculum' as something that usually exists in separate parts. A glance at many schools' timetables, especially those in secondary schools, confirms that connotation when one sees separate blocks of time labelled for particular subjects or activities. This poses a dilemma: If the natural state of curriculum is one of separation, then why integrate? Why do some educators wish to 'make whole' or 'renew' the curriculum? What do they hope to achieve by this? What does an integrated curriculum look like? What challenges does it impose on the teachers who implement it? What effect does it have on the learning of students who engage with it? What does an integrated curriculum mean for the kinds of knowledge imparted to participants, compared to a curriculum comprised of separate parts? What kinds of knowledge will prepare students to cope outside of school? And, importantly, what is the contribution of an integrated curriculum to education for global citizenship?

To answer our questions, we began an exploration of the kinds of curricula described as integrated in our location, initially Australia, and later including Canada. This book synthesizes the findings from our explorations, and in it we accept the challenge of answering these questions. Thus, the first chapter begins with an exploration of the most fundamental question: What is meant by curriculum integration? We map its territory by exploring its meanings and its roots and examine its changing popularity. Throughout this book, we draw heavily upon more than a decade of our own research and reflection, so the chapter continues with an overview of the focus and methods we have used in our research journey. We identify what is known about curriculum integration and what questions remain unanswered or equivocal. Subsequent chapters develop four issues we have found central to our thinking about curriculum integration: the variety of curriculum described as integrated, the structures that support curriculum integration, learning from an integrated curriculum, and the structure and status of knowledge.

The first issue, discussed in Chapter 2, is the variety of approaches to curriculum integration. Here we review the kinds of approaches to, or categorizations of, curriculum that are found in the literature; we outline the approaches we uncovered in our own research and illustrate these using case studies from our work. The second issue, covered in Chapter 3, concerns the school structures that support curriculum integration. Here we analyse how the nature of integration typically challenges the status quo in schooling, and identify the kinds of school structures and curriculum interests that support integration. We introduce the notion of a Worldly Perspective on curriculum to examine how the knowledge interests of curriculum integration can be balanced in a way that acknowledges the practicalities of curriculum and the challenges faced by teachers. We use this Worldly Perspective in Chapter 4 to explore the third issue, learning in integrated curriculum. We examine learning outcomes through different theoretical lenses and then analyze three arguments for integration, that is, that integration assists students to transfer knowledge, helps them to focus on big ideas, and increases motivation to learn. We explore the relationship between classroom contexts and learning, concluding that context is an important determinant of curricular outcomes. In Chapter 5 we analyse the fourth issue found to be central to curriculum integration – the structure and status of knowledge. We demonstrate that while integrated knowledge can be considered to be 'weak' and of low status, compared with disciplinary knowledge, the outcomes for students are powerful in terms of the broader understanding they gain of issues in their local environment.

We use the sixth chapter to synthesize our findings and look ahead to the way knowledge is used in the twenty-first century, and give examples of the kind of knowledge students learn at school. Throughout the book we develop an argument for what we call a Worldly Perspective on curriculum. In the seventh and final chapter, we draw together the threads of the arguments we have made to elucidate Seven key components of the Worldly Perspective and identify it as one that recognizes balance between discipline and integrated knowledge and connects global and local views. This perspective on curriculum integration, we argue, has enormous potential to foster students' knowledge that counts in our global community.

Léonie Rennie
Grady Venville
John Wallace

Acknowledgements

The research reported in this book was carried out with funding from three research grants: an Australian Research Council Collaborative Grant (C59700325) with the Education Department of Western Australia, an Australian Research Council Discovery Grant (DP0451818), and a Canadian Social Science and Humanities Research Council Standard Grant (410-2006-2443). The opinions expressed are those of the authors and should not be attributed to the funding bodies.

We greatly appreciate our colleagues who worked with us on these projects: John Malone, Rachel Sheffield, Fiona Budgen, Sheryl MacMath and Xiaohong Chi. We thank them for their insights and support. Finally, we are indebted to the teachers and students with whom we have worked over the past 15 years.

1 Mapping the territory

The background to curriculum integration

What is meant by curriculum integration?

The words 'integrate' and 'integration' derive from the Latin word *integratus*, past participle of *integrare*, meaning to make whole, to renew. Meanings of integrate include to make whole or complete by adding or bringing together parts; to put or bring (parts) together into a whole; to unify; and to give or indicate the whole, sum, or total of something. Integration has a special meaning in mathematics where, not surprisingly perhaps, the reverse process is referred to as differentiation. In terms of curriculum, however, it would seem that integration is concerned with bringing together parts of the curriculum which would otherwise be separate and differentiated.

If the term integration connotes a bringing together, just what is brought together in a curriculum described as integrated? It varies considerably. Various forms of curriculum integration have been around for more than a century and interest in it has ebbed and flowed. However, the attention given to integration in the school curriculum has escalated over the last three or four decades. For example, in their historical analysis of integrated curriculum during the twentieth century, Berlin and Lee (2005) focused on integration in the subjects of science and mathematics. They recorded only two articles published in the first two decades, both in 1905, but revealed a dramatic increase in publication from the mid 1980s. Gehrke (1998) remarked on the popularity of curriculum integration, more broadly interpreted, in the 1990s and demonstrated the increased number of publications devoted to the topic in the period 1990–1997, compared with the decades of the 1970s and the 1980s (Gehrke, 1998, Tables 1 and 2). However, there is little consistency in the character of the curriculum described as integrated. Somewhere near the height of its recent popularity, Kysilka (1998, p. 198) noted, 'At the moment it seems that integration means whatever someone decides it means, as long as there is a "connection" between previously separated content areas and/or skill areas'.

While consistent with the notion of connectedness and 'bringing together', Kysilka's note emphasizes diversity in definition. The diversity of meaning of integration is illustrated in a fairly comprehensive review of integrated curriculum in science carried out by Haggis and Adey (1979) over three decades ago, when integrated science education was a rapidly developing and expanding educational field. UNESCO initiated its book series *New Trends in Integrated Science Teaching* early in the 1970s as a reflection of this expansion, and provided considerable international funding for developing countries to prepare new curricula. Haggis and Adey (1979) collected data on 130 integrated science curricula worldwide. The criteria for inclusion in their list were that the curriculum be both trialled and published (or there was intention to publish). Only three curricula were developed at school level, 40 were developed by universities, and most of the rest developed at some administrative level in the educational system of the particular country. Many of these curricula had at least some of their material derived from other curricula and changes were made to suit the circumstances of the countries where they were to be used. Most of these curricula were described as 'integrated' because they included two or more science subjects, such as physics and chemistry, but about one-third also included a non-science subject, often described, rather vaguely, as a 'social component'. Haggis and Adey counted 37 curricula initiated in the years 1961 to 1969, and 77 in the following six years, from 1970 to 1975. They remarked on increasing attempts to include greater social relevance and environmental issues in integrated science courses, as well as attempts to interrelate integrated science courses with other curriculum areas and, more latterly, to give greater attention to curriculum evaluation in science education.

Although these trends show increasing interest in integration, the curricula reviewed by Haggis and Adey essentially amounted to the bringing together of some science subjects. Although a few of the courses were quite prescriptive, many gave teachers considerable leeway in selecting and using course (as distinct from subject) content according to the needs of their students. Haggis and Adey (1979, p. 80) identified three 'kinds of integration': a *coordinated* curriculum in which bits of the science subjects were woven together, a *combined* curriculum with separate science subjects but where the seams between them had disappeared, and an *amalgamated* curriculum where ideas from the separate sciences were called upon as they were needed to cope with problems as they arose from the environment of the learner. We can see in these three kinds of integration two key issues emerging: first, the strength or coherence of the science subject or discipline; and second, response to the needs of the learner. Most of the discussion about curriculum integration surrounds these two issues.

To see why, we need to look more closely at the nature of curriculum. However, finding a meaning for curriculum is not straightforward. As Smith and Lovat (2003, p. x) pointed out, 'curriculum is one of those words everyone thinks they understand until they hear someone else using it. It is a word with multiple meanings and different meanings in different contexts'. Teachers may mean one thing, their principals another, and the school district administrators something else entirely. All are likely to mean something quite different to what the students believe they experience. Dillon (2009, p. 343) tried to get at the 'basic things that compose curriculum' by posing a series of questions clustered according to the nature of curriculum, its elements and its practice. Scott (2008) stated that curriculum, at any of its levels, national or institutional, has four dimensions: aims or objectives, content or subject matter, methods or procedures, and evaluation or assessment. These four dimensions are immediately reminiscent of the four fundamental questions asked by Tyler (1949) in his classic text *Basic Principles of Curriculum and Instruction*. These relate to the educational purposes of the school curriculum, the educational experiences to be selected, how those experiences can be organized, and how their effectiveness in achieving their purpose can be evaluated. Tyler organized his book according to these questions, and his explication of curriculum still has relevance today. In fact, Dillon's (2009) analysis of questions about curriculum failed to find an improved scheme of questions.

A discussion about curriculum, then, might start with its educational purposes and the choice of educational experiences that might achieve them. Carr (2007, p. 5) suggested that 'an educated person is one who can make connected sense of things – not for any immediate practical purpose, but for the sake of a meaningfully unified, ordered and/or directed life'. Such a definition would not fit well with those who believe that schooling necessarily has a vocational objective and therefore its purpose should be to provide knowledge and skills that have instrumental value in a vocational sense. This distinction suggests that if the purpose of curriculum is to turn out educated persons, then participants will be served by a curriculum that offers intrinsically valuable knowledge and skills. If the purpose of the curriculum is to prepare people for employment, then participants will be served by a curriculum wherein all educational content has vocational or instrumental value. Although these extremes demonstrate that the purpose of the curriculum determines the kinds of educational experiences, in terms of both content and activities that are offered to the participants, neither extreme is a convincing representation of a 'best' curriculum. More generally acceptable would be a curriculum where the purpose was to result in educated persons who make connected sense of things and can lead meaningful and ordered lives, but who also have the knowledge and skills to cope with, or be trained for, a vocation of their choice. Such a curriculum might provide the knowledge that counts in a local and a global community, but care must be given to selecting what content and which activities are best likely to serve the needs of our youth. What might they be? What pieces of knowledge and what kinds of skills should be included in such a curriculum? What should be excluded?

These questions cannot be answered unless the educational purposes of the curriculum are clearly articulated. Then, when the answers are available, the next question becomes: how should the selected knowledge and skills be structured? This question leads to Tyler's third question of curriculum, which asks how the chosen educational experiences, the content and activities, can be organized for effective instruction.

Scott (2008) pointed out that now, in the twenty-first century, the dominant structure of school curricula is alignment with disciplines such as physics, mathematics, history and literature, and that the disciplines themselves almost always provide the structure of the curriculum. Such a structure suggests that there is established, canonical and disciplinary knowledge that is included in each subject curriculum. This is widely referred to as a disciplinary, or traditional, organization of curriculum where the kinds of knowledge selected are those that are considered essential to learning about and within the discipline. In such a curriculum, the discipline or subjects are central and the key questions to be answered are: what content needs to be learned? and how should that content be organized? But there is an alternative starting point. It begins with the question, what content does the learner need to know? This leads to a very different curriculum structure, one which is organized around the learner, a learner-centred curriculum, within which content and activities are chosen with the learner's needs in mind. How can we know what kinds of knowledge and skills the learner needs? Any reasonable answer implies that the learner needs to have a role in selecting and organizing the components of the curriculum. Further, although subject content will be involved, its selection will be dependent not on the nature or dictates of the discipline, but on the needs of the learner.

The final question of curriculum asks: how can the effectiveness of the learning experiences be evaluated? Obviously, the kinds of assessment tasks used to measure effectiveness must reflect the experiences offered to the learner that provided the opportunities to achieve the purpose of the curriculum. In a subject-centred curriculum, assessment will focus on how much of the established content has been learned. In a learner-centred curriculum, the assessment activities will be shaped by the different kinds of experiences offered, and will likely focus on outcomes other than the learning of content.

We see that there are two contrasting approaches to curriculum organization: around the discipline, resulting in a discipline-centred and, by default, a teacher-centred curriculum; or around the learner, resulting in a learner-centred curriculum. Most advocates of curriculum integration argue for a learner-centred rather than a subject- or discipline-centred curriculum. Which of these might hold most promise for providing students with knowledge that counts in a global community? If it is the former, then curriculum integration means a fundamental change in the way that most curricula have been developed for many decades. Curricula that are devised by focusing on questions about what selection of subject knowledge should be taught are instead devised by focusing on questions about the needs of students to cope with what is happening in their lives. Immediately the curriculum focus moves to serving the needs of the student and away from serving the traditions of subject knowledge.

The needs of the learner and the primacy of the subject matter are also the two issues discerned by Haggis and Adey (1979), so even 30 years ago these issues were not new. Thirty years earlier, when Tyler (1949) wrote about his questions of curriculum, he provided no answers; rather, he wrote about ways that answers might be found. Subject matter is always part of the answer, but Tyler emphasized that determining the purpose of the curriculum must include consideration of the learners' requirements. Such a view was hardly radical. Even earlier, John Dewey (1902, 1915/1900, 1916) and his contemporaries suggested that by applying ideas from one discipline to another, students would come to appreciate the interconnection of ideas and the relevance of their schooling. Dewey's ideas of curriculum held the learner's experiences central to learning, although he recognized that not all experiences were educational!

During the twentieth century there was an increasing emphasis on the disciplines of knowledge. As knowledge increased, so did belief in the value of the disciplines as a way of organising knowledge, particularly in structuring curriculum. In the 1960s, curriculum development drew upon theorists such as Bruner (1960), whose concept of curriculum was oriented about the structure of the discipline. The strength of disciplines still underpins curriculum development in Western countries, even though there may be arguments about the coherence of the disciplines themselves. There are also differences between a discipline and its school subject or subjects. In science, for example, Brown (1977) grappled with the meaning of 'integrated science' in the context of the growth in integrated science curricula that led to the Haggis and Adey (1979) review. Brown also explored the value of an integrated approach to science education, concluding that there were multiple ways in which separate science subjects were integrated into one 'science' subject, but the reasons for doing so were rarely made explicit and the value was uncertain. Thirty years later, Jenkins (2007) contributed an historical/political analysis that questioned the assumption of 'school science' as a coherent curriculum component, based on the 'notion of a unifying scientific method that continues to ignore important philosophical, conceptual, and methodological differences between the basic sciences' (pp. 265–266). Still, in most schools we have 'science', or 'general science', taught as a single school subject in the lower grades while in the higher grades, physics, chemistry and biology are taught as separate subjects.

Putting aside these contentions for the moment, and returning to the disciplines as an organizing structure for curriculum, we find that during the 1970s some educators were becoming increasingly concerned at the fragmentary nature of discipline-based curricula. There was dissatisfaction with the outcomes, particularly at the middle school level. In turn, this rejuvenated interest in the centrality of the learner and in the need to make links between the branches of knowledge represented by school subjects that were discrete in school, but were not discrete in the learner's life outside of school. Curriculum integration became more prominent as a means to resolve this dissatisfaction.

As the popularity of curriculum integration waxed into the 1970s and beyond, the varying interpretations of it, and the seeming dissonance between the needs of the disciplines and the needs of the learner, created a false dichotomy: 'the disciplines of knowledge are the enemy of curriculum integration', as Beane (1995, p. 616) quoted one educator. Beane was prompted to 'set the record straight'. In doing so, he identified the critical issue that shaped his view of curriculum integration, its implications for implementation and its outcomes. It was not that the disciplines were ignored or forgotten, but the idea that curriculum design should deal with what knowledge and skills students need to be able to cope with issues in their lives, rather than deal with the selection of subject matter that should be taught.

> Curriculum integration is not simply an organizational device requiring cosmetic changes or realignments in lesson plans across various subject areas. Rather, it is a way of thinking about what schools are for, about the sources of curriculum, and about the uses of knowledge. Curriculum integration begins with the idea that the sources of curriculum ought to be problems, issues, and concerns posed by life itself. I have argued elsewhere that such concerns fall into two spheres: 1) self- or personal concerns and 2) issues and problems posed by the larger world.
>
> (Beane, 1995, p. 616)

Beane went on to explain:

> Curriculum integration ... calls forth those ideas that are most important and powerful in the disciplines of knowledge – the ones that are most significant because they emerge in life itself. And because they are placed in the context of personally and socially significant concerns, they are more likely to have real meaning in the lives of young people, the kind of meaning they do not now have. (p. 620)

Beane's position is clear: conceived in this way, curriculum integration requires a fundamental refocusing of the purpose of curriculum; a significant departure from the established, subject-based curriculum. And yet, as we began our exploratory journey into the meaning of curriculum integration, we found that the literature was replete with examples of 'integrated' curricula, some of which did little more than match up lesson plans between subject areas. But also called 'integrated' curricula were others, much closer to Beane's description, that reflected a real change in purpose. Consequently, we started our exploration of curriculum integration with the realization that it was a slippery concept that could lead us to some interesting, but possibly frustrating, adventures.

Exploration: Our research and its methods

Our understanding of curriculum integration evolved from research carried out over 15 years and associated with three major funded studies. It is convenient to consider our explorations in three stages. In the first stage, during a project funded from 1997 to 1999, our purpose was to survey the kinds of curricula being enacted in Western Australian classrooms that were described as integrated by the teachers involved. We completed six major case studies and six minor case studies, or 'snapshots', using classroom observations, document analyses, and extensive interviews with teachers, students and administrators. An overview of these studies is given in Table 1.1 and more complete details are available in the Appendix, where schools are listed alphabetically by the pseudonyms used throughout the book. Stage Two of our research began when a new funding was received for research in Australian schools from 2004 to 2006. In Stage Two we revisited nine of the Stage One case studies to see what had happened in the interim. We also explored, via interviews with teachers, six other instances of curriculum integration. Table 1.1 includes an overview of the Stage Two research activities. Armed with this knowledge of curriculum integration in the mid 2000s, we undertook Stage Three. Eight further case studies, including three funded Canadian case studies, resulted from using similar research methods as for Stage One. The overview of Stage Three appears in Table 1.1 and details of the case studies are included in the Appendix. The findings from all three stages provide the primary data for this book and, together with our continuing reflections over this lengthy journey, enable us to provide an informed analysis of the potential of integrated curriculum to produce the kind of knowledge that can help students to cope in a global community.

Stage One: Case studies of integrated practice

We began our research in 1997, at a time when there was considerable pressure for reform in the middle years of schooling for young adolescents. A recent Australian report (Eyers, 1992, p. 16) had pointed out 'there are clear signs of social alienation and lack of educational success among these [10- to 15-year-old] students to the extent that their education and positive development is of real concern in a number of countries, including Australia'. In the light of emerging evidence that middle-year students may be better served by an integrated curriculum, reserving subject specialization for the more senior years, the Education Department of Western Australia had begun to promote a middle-school culture in several new schools. At the same time, a new state-wide curriculum was in development, with outcomes to be articulated in eight traditional learning areas, entitled English, Science, Mathematics, Society and Environment, Languages other than English, Art, Health Education, and Technology and Enterprise (Curriculum Council of Western Australia, 1998).

Table 1.1 Summary of the research programme

Stage and date	Purpose	Focus	Data collection
Stage One 1997–1999	Provide a research base to inform the development and implementation of integrated curriculum models, document best practice and develop exemplars	Six major case studies	School visits, classroom observation, document analysis, interviews
		Six minor case studies or 'snapshots'	Document analysis, interviews
Stage Two 2004	Part One: Determine reasons for integration, what helped and hindered implementation, and what determined longevity	'Revisits' to nine of the Stage One schools	Secondary analysis of Stage One data, teacher interviews
	Part Two: Test synthesis of enabling and inhibiting factors that impacted implementation of integrated curriculum	Six new case studies	Teacher interviews
Stage Three 2005–2008	Explore the outcomes for students; what are the cognitive and affective gains?	Eight new case studies	School visits, classroom observation, document analysis, interviews

Middle-school teachers wishing to integrate curricula had to deal with sets of outcomes from several learning areas but had little guidance on how to do this. Consequently, our intention was to provide a research base to inform the development and implementation of integrated curriculum models, to examine and document 'best practice' in relation to integrated curriculum delivery in middle schools, and to develop exemplars of teaching practice which led to students' learning in integrated contexts.

We began Stage One with an Australian Research Council Collaborative Grant (1997–1999) in which we partnered with the Education Department of Western Australia. We focused on the three subject areas of science, mathematics and technology and looked for examples of integration in the middle-school years, which we defined as Years 7 to 9, approximately ages 11 to 15 years. Programmes were selected for attention in primary schools (in Western Australia primary schools serve students in Years Kindergarten to 7), secondary schools (Years 8 to 12), country high schools (Years K to 10), private schools (Years K to 12), and two new middle schools (Years 7 to 9). We began with description, using school visits, teacher interviews, analysis of teacher materials and students' work samples, to develop 'snapshots' of programmes in schools. On the basis of these findings, we selected six school situations for more intensive study, involving classroom observations and interviews with students as well as teachers. An overview of all case studies is presented in the Appendix. Using pseudonyms, we provide brief descriptions of each school and its programme and our means of data collection.

The main outcome of this work was a case book of exemplars for teachers (Venville, Wallace, Rennie and Malone, 1999a), comprising some general information about integration, descriptions of programmes described as integrated and analyses of the facilitating and inhibiting factors that affected their success or otherwise. These exemplars were made available as resources on the Education Department's website. In addition, a series of conference presentations and journal articles made our findings available to more academic audiences. Some of these were descriptive of individual programmes, such as Venville, Wallace, Rennie and Malone (1999b), which described an integrated bridge-building activity at Southern High School that is a focus of Chapter 5. As we pondered the data and the outcomes and began to think beyond the immediate case studies, more abstract analyses of our findings resulted in further papers, such as Wallace, Rennie, Malone and Venville (2001), which synthesized our findings in a generic sense and looked forward to what further questions needed to be asked and answered, and Venville, Wallace, Rennie and Malone (2002), which documented our research so far and, among other things, identified the status and associated power of discipline knowledge as a major barrier to curriculum integration.

Stage Two: Identifying conditions favouring integration

While the intentions in Stage One of our research were essentially pragmatic, by Stage Two we had many unanswered questions about the nature of curriculum integration. What precipitated its implementation in schools as an innovation or intervention? What helped and what hindered that implementation? What factors affected its longevity? Stage Two was funded by an Australian Research Council Discovery Project for the years 2004 to 2006. We were keen to re-survey the curriculum integration landscape in Western Australia because we had become aware that its popularity had faded, as indeed the desire for separate middle schools had faded. Our first task, therefore, was to revisit the schools that provided our case studies in Stage One to see what had happened in the intervening seven years. We conducted a secondary analysis of the data from nine of these twelve schools, those for which we had the most complete data sets, and attempted to identify and itemise conditions that we considered had been enabling or inhibiting in each of their integration programmes. We contacted these schools again to obtain information about the current state of the programme we had examined previously. Due to staff-turnover in the intervening period, we were able to find the same teacher(s) or another staff member who was familiar with the earlier programme in only seven of the nine schools. Via interviews with these teachers we consolidated our secondary analysis with the new information obtained for the current state of their integration programmes.

In the second part of Stage Two we sought a broader data base to test and refine our synthesis of the enabling and inhibiting factors that impacted integration programmes. We approached six practising middle-school teachers, three male and three female, from metropolitan and rural locations, each of whom had current or recent experience in teaching an integrated curriculum. Face-to-face, hour-long interviews were conducted with five of these teachers, and the sixth was interviewed by telephone for reasons of geographical location. We asked about the teachers' histories of involvement with integrated programmes and their identification of the factors which they found to impede or facilitate their attempts at integration. Using the data from both parts of Stage Two, we were able to postulate a set of key programme characteristics that might predict the success or otherwise of attempts at integration (Wallace, Sheffield, Rennie and Venville, 2007) and these are discussed in some depth in Chapter 3 of this volume.

Stage Three: New case studies focusing on learning outcomes

Stage One raised numerous issues for us in terms of understanding integration as it was practised in Western Australian schools. In Stage Two we explored what happened from the teachers' point of view, the inhibiting and enabling factors and the facilitating conditions that augured well for successful integration. In Stage Three we returned to an exploration of the outcomes for students. What were they learning in terms of both affective and cognitive gains? We embarked upon a new series of case studies, using similar methods as in Stage One for our data collection: school visits, interviews with teachers and students, classroom (and in some cases out-of-classroom) observations of students' activities, and analysis of various documents produced by teachers and by students. We were able also to conduct some case studies in Canada, funded by the Social Science and Humanities Research Council (2006–2008), which provided additional contexts for integration. Details of the eight new case studies are included in the Appendix.

Each of the eight Stage Three case studies had unique features and consequently the outcomes of each were analysed from a different perspective. The outcomes not only provided an array of student outcomes, but also provided a context in which the findings from Stage Two could be used to examine the reasons for the relative success or otherwise of the integrated programmes. Several cross-case analyses, such as Venville, Sheffield, Rennie and Wallace (2008), compared and contrasted the implementation of the intended curriculum integration programmes and demonstrated how the outcomes were affected by various aspects of school context. We have continued to work with our data as we try to understand further the nature of curriculum integration as it appeared in our case study schools. For example, we have argued the advantages of theoretical triangulation as a way of understanding the notion of balance in integrated curriculum (Rennie, Venville and Wallace, 2011).

Key findings and questions about curriculum integration

Following our first series of case studies, we synthesized our findings and speculations in a paper entitled 'What We Know and What We Need to Know about Curriculum Integration in Science, Mathematics and Technology' (Wallace *et al.*, 2001). At that time, we suggested that integration is an ideological stance underpinned by mostly epistemological assumptions, variously contested by proponents and opponents of curriculum integration. We knew that integration came in various forms that were implemented with varying degrees of commitment and with varying life-spans. We proposed that integration challenged what Tylack and Tobin (1994) called the 'grammar of schooling', that is, the culture, customs, ceremonies and artefacts of everyday life within schools, including the tradition of organising the curriculum around subjects. We had also found that the success of integration was often idiosyncratic, dependent on the educational contexts and the motivations and aims of the participants. It seemed to us that curriculum integration involved both losses and gains in terms of the learning by students and the efforts of teachers. There remained issues that required answers. During our research, we often were not sure what purpose the curriculum integration was intended to serve. What problem was it addressing? How was it addressing that problem? We needed to know much more about what students were learning in integrated settings and how that compared with what they might learn in a different curriculum. We needed to know whether or not, and how, successful integration projects could be sustained and scaled up over time. We thought that these latter points were tied up with the contexts for integration, the grammar of schooling and the nature of knowledge.

A decade later, we were able to reflect on and update those wonderings in the context of our more recent studies. Earlier, our research had focused on integrated curriculum involving science, mathematics and technology; now, after considerable further research, we are able to broaden our perspective to other subject areas. Overall, we believe there are four issues that are central to understanding what is meant by curriculum integration and underpin the success of its implementation, the nature of its outcomes and its longevity. These four issues are addressed in Chapters 2 to 5, respectively. They are the nature of integration, implementing curriculum integration, learning in integrated curriculum settings and the status of school knowledge.

The nature of integration

We discovered very early in our research that 'integrated' curricula come in many guises. Although each of the curricula we examined was described by its initiators as 'integrated', there were few commonalities. Not surprisingly, given the importance of the place of knowledge in curriculum, these could be distinguished according to the degree to which the traditional boundaries of the school subjects were preserved. Sometimes the subjects did not change; they remained separate, but similar concepts were taught in a synchronous or correlated way to enhance a particular curriculum theme. Such curricula have been described as multidisciplinary (Drake, 1993; Jacobs, 1989), because although the ideas might be correlated they are treated within the context of the separate disciplines, usually within the normal school timetable. In some integrated curricula, which might be described as interdisciplinary, content might be altered to allow teachers to focus on a theme, perhaps with associated timetable changes to allow students to see greater connections among the content of the different subject areas. Other times the boundaries became blurred, or even disappeared, where the concepts from several subjects were called upon to focus on a particular project or to explore solutions to a problem. In these cases, which have been described as transdisciplinary (Drake, 1993; Jacobs, 1989), the needs and interests of the learner become much more important in selecting content. In Chapter 2 of this volume we explore the meaning of integration and describe examples of our own case studies to illustrate the diversity of curriculum integration we found in our research.

Implementing curriculum integration

The variety of forms of curriculum integration, the amount of effort required of teachers to mount and maintain their integrated curriculum and the transitory existence of some of them, drew our attention to the inherent barriers to the implementation of integrated curriculum. At its root, curriculum integration challenges the grammar of schooling (Tylack and Tobin, 1994). The everyday life of a school, particularly a secondary school, is ordered around routines and traditions, the customary ways of structuring schooling, many of which are associated with the teaching of school subjects. Streaming of classes, use of subject-specialist teachers who gather in their own subject departments, organization of school timetables and content-based summative assessment procedures, all work to protect the boundaries of individual subjects. In some of our later case studies we tested the ideas formed earlier about the issues involved in implementing and sustaining an integrated curriculum (Wallace *et al.*, 2007) and our findings and suggestions are discussed in Chapter 3. In particular, we introduce the notion of a Worldly Perspective, a view of curriculum that recognizes the legitimacy of different approaches and interests and their contribution to knowledge. We argue the need for flexible school structures able to respond to the needs of teachers and students, together with a more balanced and pragmatic approach to integrated curricula.

Learning in integrated curriculum settings

There are still major arguments about the value of what it is that students learn in integrated contexts. The use of traditional forms of assessment, focusing on content learning of specific subjects, has validity in traditional, subject-differentiated curricula, but when curricula are integrated, different kinds of knowledge and skills are valued and different kinds of assessment must be employed to enable students to demonstrate what they know and can do. The assessment of students' learning in integrated contexts, and demonstrating its value, has presented problems for most educators who attempt to implement curriculum integration. We have found it useful to consider learning in terms of different theoretical lenses, different arguments for integration and different contexts in which integration can occur. The approach elaborated in Chapter 4 leads to a more nuanced view of student learning in integrated settings than is generally found in the literature.

The status of school knowledge

A decade ago, we observed 'that integration is an idea or stance about curriculum underpinned by certain ideological assumptions' (Wallace *et al.*, 2001, p. 10). We thought then, and it stills seems to be the case, that most of the arguments about curriculum integration, both for and against, 'turn on an epistemological axis'. Proponents, like Beane (1995) quoted earlier, argue that knowledge in integrated curricula is about the problems, issues and concerns posed by life itself. Knowledge is worthwhile according to the use that can be made of it in coping with, and understanding, issues in everyday life. Opponents argue that worthwhile knowledge resides in robust understandings of the nature and concepts of the disciplines, like history, science and mathematics, and being able to use that knowledge in the ways of the discipline (Hatch, 1998). The discussion in Chapter 5 is devoted to the nature, structure and status of knowledge as central to a consideration of integrated curriculum. As in our other chapters, we draw on examples from our case studies to illustrate the points being made.

Moving forward and looking to the future

In the second decade of the twenty-first century, it has become increasingly significant that we live in a connected world. The era of social networking via hand-held devices makes a difference to how students communicate with each other, both in terms of content and how language is used. The educational context continues to change and what we do for our students in school matters. There are continuing pressures for revision of curriculum, pressures from theoreticians who explore the changing nature of knowledge and what this means for curriculum and assessment (Kelly, Luke and Green, 2008). Educators, such as Aikenhead (2006), who argue for a more humanist and meaningful curriculum, and parents and students themselves, increasingly, are demanding a schooling experience that they perceive to be worthwhile and relevant to solve challenges in today's changing world. In Chapter 6 we explore how knowledge is used and the kinds of knowledge to which students have access through their school curriculum. Using the Worldly Perspective on curriculum, we argue that worthwhile and powerful knowledge comes from a curriculum that balances disciplinary and integrated knowledge and connects local and global views about knowledge. Finally, in Chapter 7, we draw together our discussion of knowledge and curriculum; we enumerate seven key components of the Worldly Perspective as a means of describing the curriculum that can provide our students with knowledge that counts.

The concept of curricula that are balanced, in terms of knowledge sources, and connected, in terms of working from local to global knowledge, is not the everyday view of curriculum structure. Clark (1997) has argued strongly that our educational vision must change if we are to help students to cope with the future.

> Our educational vision/mission must be one in which *teachers and students are working cooperatively to insure that every student who graduates is functionally literate, that is, they are prepared to respond deliberately and creatively to the demands of economic necessity, enlightened and informed social responsibility, and qualified planetary citizenship.*
>
> (Clark, 1997, p. 51, original emphasis)

Functional literacy, in Clark's view, includes

> flexibility, transferability of skills, proficiency in anticipating problems, an aptitude for knowing more with less information, the capacity to improvise by making decisions without enough information, a willingness to do more and be satisfied with less, tolerance for and the ability to work and live cooperatively in the midst of diversity, change, ambiguity, uncertainty, and paradox, a high level of self-direction and personal discipline, and skill in listening carefully, articulating clearly, and resolving conflicts peacefully. Finally, functional literacy must include the capacity to consciously and deliberately create personal and collective visions of desired futures and the competencies necessary to make those futures manifest. This is a tall order.
> (pp. 51–52)

This is a tall order indeed. But who would not wish their children to be educated to the level of functional literacy Clark describes? Surely this would require the kind of curriculum that might provide knowledge that counts in a global community? Clark envisions such a curriculum as a learner-centred, integrated curriculum which begins with the assumption of 'the connectedness of things'. Such a curriculum, according to Clark (1997, p. 73), gives priority to context over content; concepts over facts; questions over answers; imagination over knowledge; intuition over rational logic; developmental intent over graded content; the learning process over the product of learning; and quality of information over quantity of information. Put this way, Clark's vision does not seem to be out of reach, and yet we find ourselves in a place where many school curricula do not reflect such characteristics. Moving closer to them requires a much better understanding of the issues we have identified as critical to curriculum integration: the variety of integrated curricula and the challenges they offer to school structures, arguments about students' learning and structure of knowledge. Throughout this book we examine these issues and explore how a balanced, connected curriculum can help to provide our students with knowledge that counts. First, however, we turn to a description of the nature of integrated curriculum.

2 The nature of curriculum integration

Connection and approaches

In the opening chapter, we drew attention to the connectedness of our increasingly global world. The theme of connectedness underpins Clark's (1997) suggestion that, to help students cope with their futures, our educational vision should be one that enables students to become functionally literate, to become people who are flexible, self-disciplined and can anticipate and solve problems. Such a vision, Clark argued, would require a learner-centred, integrated curriculum. Proponents of an integrated curriculum view connectedness as a central tenet, as is evident in the writings of Drake (1993) and others. The nature of curriculum integration, as described in the educational literature, is quite diverse, and we begin this chapter with a synthesis of some of the significant issues. In our research, we also found considerable diversity in the kinds of curriculum integration implemented by the schools we visited. From an exploration of participants' perceptions of the purposes they serve and the programmes that resulted, we devised a framework into which our experiences of curriculum integration could be structured. In this chapter we use a case study to illustrate each element of this framework. With this framework as a base, the factors that affect the implementation and outcomes of the various forms of integrated curricula are explored in the subsequent chapter.

The nature of curriculum integration

Clark (1997, p. 70) proposed that 'an integrated curriculum begins with an assumption of the "connectedness of things"', and further, that 'an integrated curriculum is learner-centred. Learning is "meaning-making"'. To make meaning, we must make connections between things, by making patterns, organizing experiences, and creating 'meaningful wholes'. However, people must make their own meaning; in other words, each person is responsible for his or her own learning. Clark (1997, p. 71) also emphasized the importance of context as 'the frame of reference that provides meaning'. To assist learners to learn, then, there must be context, or a reference framework, that has relevance to learners to assist them in meaning-making; a way of connecting what the learners know to a bigger, more global picture.

The notion of connectedness underpins our understanding of curriculum integration; connectedness in terms of connections between the things to be learned, and connectedness to the learner to enable him or her to make meaning of those things. This is reminiscent of the two foci in discussions about curriculum integration. One is the internal coherence of the subjects or disciplines around which curricula are frequently organized, and the other is the needs of the learner. Disciplines reflect different perspectives of the world; therefore, to achieve connectedness between them, Clark (1997, p. 39) stated, 'an integrated curriculum must bridge the extensive network of chasms that exist among the various academic disciplines'. In other words, their different perspectives must be regarded as complementary, rather than separate, for interconnections to be made between them. Further, Clark argued, an 'integrated curriculum must also bridge the chasm that currently exists between the classroom and the world beyond its doors'. Clearly, a curriculum that can bridge that chasm will be providing a context (and a connectedness) that is relevant and meaningful to the learners and hence can assist them to make the connections that promote meaning-making.

However, bridging the chasms between the disciplines, between school and the outside world, and between the local and global communities, is not easy to do. This helps to explain why, as we quickly discovered when we began our research, so many variations shelter beneath the umbrella term of curriculum integration. It also explains why some educators are willing to describe as integrated any curricula where there is some attempt to break down the boundaries between the disciplines. Indeed, the term 'interdisciplinary curriculum' is sometimes used interchangeably with the term 'integrated curriculum', and this can become rather confusing.

Books about curriculum integration frequently refer to interdisciplinary curriculum. For example, Jacobs' (1989) popular book is entitled *Interdisciplinary Curriculum: Design and Implementation*, but she writes about a range of approaches to curriculum integration under this title. Jacobs drew on Meeth (1978, p. 10) for definitions of interdisciplinary studies. Although Meeth's context was programmes in tertiary education, his definitions are consistent with meanings used more generally, so it is helpful to report them here. Meeth (and others) considered four separate degrees or stages of going beyond a single disciplinary (or intra-disciplinary) programme. In cross-disciplinary programmes one discipline is viewed from the perspective of another, such as the physics of music. Such programmes are usually easy to develop because the teachers tend to stay in their own field and the curriculum does not disturb the structure of their discipline. Multi-disciplinary programmes include several disciplines focused on a single problem or issue, with each discipline contributing a different perspective. Again, teachers tend to stay in their own disciplines and there is no attempt to integrate those perspectives, so any integrating or synthesizing of ideas has to be done by the students. Interdisciplinary programmes, in contrast, 'attempt to integrate the contributions of several disciplines to a problem, issue or theme from life'. Here, 'integration means bringing interdependent parts of knowledge into harmonious relationship'. The boundaries between disciplines are blurred. Meeth (1978, p. 10) considers transdisciplinary programmes to be the highest level of integrated study. Such programmes start with the problem or issue and bring the appropriate disciplines to bear through a problem-solving approach. This is the most difficult to teach because teachers must know and students must learn not only how to solve problems, but also where to find the disciplinary knowledge required to solve them. Meeth (1978, p. 10) pointed out then, and it remains true today, that 'teachers need to be resource persons, broadly acquainted with many fields or thoroughly grounded in knowledge theory. Consequently, very few institutions attempt transdisciplinary study, even though it is the most common approach to the major issues that confront society'. (It will become evident that this latter point is particularly important in the context of globalization.)

We can see that Meeth's explication of interdisciplinary studies is concerned mainly with what happens to the disciplines. It is only the transdisciplinary programme where subject boundaries are really dissolved and the learner's interests and needs can become the focus of curriculum structure. The various ways of dealing with the academic disciplines have been used by some educators to create a continuum of curriculum integration, based on progression in breaking down the boundaries between them. Drake (1993) structured her three-framework continuum quite simply, taking the terms multidisciplinary, interdisciplinary and transdisciplinary as frameworks, with meanings rather similar to those given by Meeth (1978) but more clearly explained in the context of schooling. Jacobs (1989) used an extended continuum, beginning with 'parallel discipline designs'. Here, teachers of different subjects sequence topics so that similar material is taught in parallel so there is reinforcement, but subject areas remain distinct. Jacobs then described 'complementary discipline units', similar to the descriptions of multidisciplinary courses, and 'interdisciplinary units/courses' as her second and third 'degrees' of integration, both of which maintain the structure of the disciplines in some measure. More overlap between the disciplines occurs in the 'integrated day', where a theme-based programme is focused on students' interests. Finally, there is the 'complete programme', the highest level of integration, where students determine their own curriculum according to their needs and interests.

Another continuum is provided by Kysilka (1998, p. 204) who condensed a range of authors' ideas, including those of Drake and Jacobs, to offer four stages of integrated curriculum. At one end, termed 'separate disciplines', there is no integration. The second stage, 'discipline-based', is consistent with Drake's notion of multi-disciplinary or Jacobs' complementary course, where there is merely correlation of perspectives from different disciplines. Next is the 'interdisciplinary' stage, which considers students' interests and broad themes, requiring pairing or teams of teachers as discipline boundaries become blurred. The final stage is 'total integration', which is in line with Meeth's and

Drake's notion of transdisciplinary and Jacobs' view of the complete programme. In 'total integration' the learner's interests are central and the discipline boundaries dissolved.

Such continua are easy to find and they are variously helpful. Some educators have characterized a series of categories on a continuum. Texts aimed at practitioners by Fogarty (1991, 2002, for example) are built around ten models of integration with different degrees of subject overlap or restructuring of curricula (see Fogarty, 1991, for a concise description of these models). Her models were sequenced from a fragmented, subject-based model to one that immerses the learner in a curriculum where subject boundaries are not evident. Similarly, Marsh (1993) proposed a continuum beginning with 'discipline-based options' which, with increasing overlap of subjects/disciplines and school organization, eventually became 'whole school integration'. Other more simple categorizations include correlated, shared and reconstructed (Applebee, Adler and Flihan, 2007) curricula. All of these continua demonstrate a graduation from the naturally bounded school subjects as the starting point for organizing the curriculum, to a position in which the curriculum is organized around 'real world' problems, issues or projects of relevance to the learners with the subject structures broken down.

One problem we find with the notion of continua is the implicit suggestion that moving along a continuum represents progress to a more desirable state; that more integration is better, for example. However, our research demonstrates that while approaches to curriculum may be different, there is no inherent quality of 'betterness'; rather, the effectiveness of each must be judged according to its purpose. Hargreaves, Earl and Ryan (1996) pointed out that a continuum does not capture the complexity of integration and argued instead for a pragmatic position that acknowledges and incorporates many different forms of integration. Our research revealed that such a pragmatic view better reflects the broad spectrum of implemented curricula that we have observed. We have suggested a broad, inclusive description of integrated curriculum. In our view, an integrated curriculum enables students to look towards multiple dimensions that reflect the realities of their experiences outside and inside school (Venville, Rennie and Wallace, in press).

While such a broad description encompasses the range of 'integrated' curricula that we have seen, it also includes many programmes found in the literature that bear other names. A partial list includes authentic tasks (e.g., Lee and Songer, 2003); community connections (e.g., Bouillion and Gomez, 2001); contextualized instruction (e.g., Rivet and Krajcik, 2008); democratic schools (e.g., Apple and Beane, 1999); futures studies (e.g., Lloyd and Wallace, 2004); holistic education (e.g., Miller, 2007); place-based education (e.g., Gruenewald and Smith, 2008); science, technology, society and the environment (e.g., Pedretti, 2005); and youth-centred perspectives (e.g., Buxton, 2006). The common element is that students are led to look towards multiple dimensions that reflect the real world while drawing from the strengths offered by the subject disciplines. The approach to bringing those subject disciplines together is fundamental to the degree of integration that occurs, and how the organization of the curriculum can best be described.

Approaches to integrating the curriculum

Curricula vary in terms of the focus of integration, that is, the organizing structure that determines how the curriculum is put together. Most examples of the continua we discussed in this chapter focused on how the disciplines were arranged within the curriculum. Focus on the needs of the learner did not seem to become central until the highest level of integration was addressed. It is also possible that an integrated curriculum can vary in terms of extent. It can vary from one teacher in a single classroom providing a coherent, integrated programme to his/her students, to several teachers planning together for their cluster of classes, to a whole school effort with the integrated curriculum planned jointly by all teachers across all class levels.

Although the needs of the learner and the coherence of the disciplines seemed to be the two central foci for curriculum organization that we found in the literature, we found from our observations that curriculum integrators did not think about these foci in the same way. Terms such as multidisciplinary and transdisciplinary were not used by teachers in our research, although the term interdisciplinary was sometimes used. Jacobs (1989) pointed out that although Meeth's (1978) definitions might aid clarity in thinking, she also found that teachers did not use these terms, so, apart from 'interdisciplinary', Jacobs chose not to use them either. Nevertheless, the teachers in our case study schools did believe that their integration attempts benefited their students, and some also thought that an integrated approach was a more realistic way to learn about things outside of school. What guided them, however, was the way that the integrated curriculum could be fitted into their school context. In other words, final decisions about the implementation of integrated curricula were more likely to be pragmatic than idealistic.

We considered various ways to describe the range of approaches to curriculum integration we found in our research. Terms that focused on either the degree to which discipline boundaries were breached or the extent of centrality of the learner did not seem to fit, and certainly did not mesh with how teachers described what they were doing. Consequently, we decided to use terms that carried a sense of how the curricula were structured, not only in terms of the disciplines but in how they were implemented in the schools. We have chosen this way to describe approaches to integrated curricula because it seemed fruitful and inclusive of the case studies in our research. The terms we use are synchronized, thematic, project-based, cross-curricular, school-specialized and community-focused.

In the next sections we describe and provide examples of each of these approaches to curriculum integration. The examples are chosen from our case studies which are described in the Appendix, and those selected are overviewed in Table 2.1. Pseudonyms are used for all schools and teachers. The six approaches are broadly sequenced in terms of whether the subjects are taught separately or together, but there is considerable overlap among them; none can be regarded as a 'pure' form of curriculum integration. In describing these approaches to curriculum integration, we emphasize that this order is one of convenience; no hierarchy is intended. There is no suggestion that one form is somehow 'better' than another or that this is an exhaustive list of possible descriptors. Often they are the best response teachers could make in their circumstances.

Synchronized approach

Synchronized approaches focus on the coming together of specific skills, knowledge or understandings that are part of more than one subject or discipline area. Under this approach, there is a correlation between parts of the curriculum that remain separately taught, although often at similar times. This is an example of a multidisciplinary approach where the connections are planned in advance and made clear by the teachers. Typically, it involves teachers from different subject areas identifying points of connection between pre-existing topics, explicitly drawing the links and teaching in a similar manner, sometimes using common tasks or assignments. For example, in one of our Stage Three case studies, at Beachville Public School, a synchronized approach was taken in science and geography when the teachers of these subjects were both dealing with units in electricity and energy use. They planned the content of their units, identified specific links between the content in each subject area and ensured that these connections were taught in parallel. Even though there were more science than geography lessons during the 6-week period, the synchronized approach worked well, enabling students to make connections between what they were learning in the different classrooms. We revisit aspects of the Beachville case study in later chapters. Here, we provide an exemplar of the synchronized approach, using our Stage One case study of Redwood High School.

Redwood High School

Redwood was a large secondary school catering for Years 8 to 12 located in an established urban area. It had a class of academically talented students in each of Years 8, 9 and 10, and although teachers of these able students felt that they should be challenged in all subject areas, at the time of our visits only science and mathematics were taught at an advanced level. Ms McKenzie, the mathematics teacher, and Mr Doust, the science teacher, realized that there were ways to strengthen the links between these two subjects via the investigations that were required by the state curriculum in each subject.

Table 2.1 Summary of case studies used as exemplars of approaches to curriculum integration

Approach to integration	School pseudonym	Description of integrated programme
Synchronized	Beachville Public School	For a Year 9 applied class, the geography and science teachers collaborated to teach the 5-week energy topic separately but in parallel. In geography and in science, cross-curricular links and concepts were reinforced.
	Redwood High School	In the Year 8–10 academic extension programme, the science and mathematics teachers identified areas of curriculum overlap and taught integrated investigations twice a term.
Thematic	Riverview Ladies College	The five Year 8 teachers worked as a team to run integrated projects (e.g., environmental theme day) incorporating aspects of all learning areas.
	Greenbelt Community College	The Year 7, 8 and 9 teachers worked collaboratively in learning teams to design, implement and assess interdisciplinary modules (e.g., my heritage, patterns in life) leading to disciplinary and interdisciplinary outcomes.
Project-based	Southern High School	The Year 9 technology class was set a bridge-building project which incorporated knowledge of science, mathematics, engineering, design and construction. The aesthetics of the bridge were judged by the English teacher.
	Eagleton Senior High School	The science, mathematics and technology teachers worked as a team to teach the Years 8–10 academic extension programme through integrated technology-based projects (e.g., design of a solar-powered boat).
Cross-curricular	Hedgerow Primary School	Technology was an integrating subject across the curriculum, with students' design-and-make projects linked into other subject areas such as social studies, art and science, and the enterprise aspect linked to other subjects such as mathematics and literacy.
	Seaview Community School	A school-wide literary focus aimed at assisting students to learn English, which underpinned all subject areas, was supported by cross-curricular initiatives, such as horticulture relating to the school garden.
School-specialized	Oceanside High School	This coastal high school developed a marine studies specialization. Teachers in each of the 'core' subject areas taught one specified unit of marine studies in each of Years 8 to 10.
Community-focused	Kentish Middle School	A learning community of 120 Year 6 and 7 students undertook a 10-week, extensive study of the local wetland with an integrated approach involving study of water quality, land use, recycling, ecology and economics.
	Chelsea Primary School	Two combined Year 4 to 7 classes worked closely with a wildlife centre on a programme aimed at understanding, and living with, tiger snakes. All subjects were involved and the 8-week long programme culminated in a community presentation by students.

Development of the synchronized programme

At the end of the year before our visit, Ms McKenzie and Mr Doust developed concept charts of their separate subject programmes so that they could identify where integration could occur, and these formed the basis of the planning for the coming year. They met to discuss and plan what they could do with their academically talented students as a group. They decided to focus on the investigation part of the curriculum where students usually worked individually or in small groups to complete an independently researched topic.

Once or twice each term, the students were involved in an integrated mathematics and science investigation. Examples included an investigation of pendulums with the Year 8 class, in which common concepts from mathematics and science were dealt with in parallel by Ms McKenzie and Mr Doust. Another investigation involved road traffic congestion at a local street intersection that involved students developing and testing an hypothesis about the causes of congestion. In both mathematics and science, students used the same framework for designing and writing up their investigations and this contributed to continuity across the learning areas. In another investigation for Year 10s related to genetics, Ms McKenzie taught about probability and Mr Doust taught punnet squares at the same time to assist students to make connections between the mathematics and science involved in genetic inheritance.

Outcomes of the synchronized programme

The students in each class built up their own portfolio of the work they had done, including tests and other work pieces relating to the investigations, and making notes that reflected their learning. The portfolios were used so successfully that they became more widespread in the mathematics department. The school administration was supportive of the integrated programme because the students were high achievers. Although both Ms McKenzie and Mr Doust were happy with the outcomes of the integration and both were competent in their own subject field, they felt that a stronger programme could have been organized if someone with expertise in both mathematics and science were available. They considered that such joint expertise would have been valuable in seeing how links between the two subjects could best be made and a more integrated programme could flow more naturally.

Thematic approach

A thematic approach to curriculum integration employs an encompassing local or global topic or theme into which specific subject areas can be linked. The theme is usually selected in advance by groups of teachers to run for a set period, perhaps just a few weeks or a term. Typically, this is a multidisciplinary approach where the subjects are taught separately in different classrooms, but in a complementary way, with teachers and students expected to make the connections back to the theme. Sometimes classes are brought together for a culminating thematic event, such as an excursion or a special day of activities when work is shared or displayed. Usually the thematic connections are explicit and well planned, but they may come about from opportunistic events, such as a local festival. Either way, thematic approaches provide occasions for school communities to share common language and understandings around a multidisciplinary big idea. At Riverview Ladies College, one of our Stage One case studies, five teachers worked as a team to teach English, science, social studies and mathematics to all four classes of Year 8 students. Although each subject was taught separately, teachers sometimes used a thematic approach to integrated projects. One example was an environmental theme day. The students went on an excursion to the nearby river foreshore and worked on activities from each subject area which were then written up back at school. A more detailed example of the thematic approach comes from Greenbelt Community College, a middle school forming one of our Stage One major case studies.

Greenbelt Community College

Greenbelt Community College was only three years old when we visited. It had been designed as a middle school to cater in an educationally responsive way to the needs of adolescents in a rapidly growing outer metropolitan area. The foundation principal and deputy principals consulted with the local community to develop a school purpose statement that expressed commitment to learning, excellence, equity and care. The school enrolled students from Years 7 to 9 and the overall vision for curriculum development was to facilitate a gradual movement from a generalized course in Year 7 to subject specialization in Year 10, when students moved to the nearby senior school.

Development of the thematic programme

An integrated approach was planned for Years 7, 8 and 9 by designing modules of work in each area around cross-curricular themes. Teachers were given time to collaborate and use their expertise in their subject areas to plan a series of modules that could be repeated in alternate years so that students would cover all learning outcomes. This ensured coverage of the curriculum in all subject areas and provided students with a full range of choice in subject pathways when they entered the senior school. The modules were not designed to be prescriptive, but served as guidelines for teachers to structure their programmes of work in sufficiently flexible ways to serve the needs of their students.

The theme of each integrated module was used to suggest concepts and foci for each of the eight learning areas from the local curriculum guidelines.

For example, the 'My Heritage' module included aspects of subjects that enabled students to reflect on their own genetic heritage but also their cultural heritage. In mathematics, for example, suggested concepts included 3-D shapes in the past and present, locations and paths – topology and simple navigation. In science the emphasis was on Australia and its changing natural environment, with students researching famous Australian scientists and investigating the long-term effects of tree-felling on the natural environment, including agriculture and native flora and fauna. The subject of health and physical education included students learning about the history of sport, ethnic and cultural influences on food and health, and the nature of childhood diseases and vaccination. Biographical reading and writing were central to the focus in English, including use of old correspondence and so on. Genealogy and students' family trees were developed in social studies and features of the programme were community visits to senior citizen centres and invitations to elders to visit the school. In the arts, students looked at Australian theatre and the impact of radio and television on society. Thus each subject worked around the My Heritage theme, and although there were overlapping topics and some joint work by teachers, such as team-teaching, the subjects tended to remain separate. Overall, students studied a strongly themed, multidisciplinary programme.

Outcomes of the thematic programme

Each module was focused on a culminating theme day, which was designed to highlight the integrated curriculum and the flexibility in planning. Often, visitors from the community and members of the school's administrative team participated in the theme days and students exhibited both individual and group work. Other times, an excursion was organized. One teacher recalled her personal highlight of the programme as the theme day accompanying the My Heritage module. Students performed plays and read their stories about the First World War, the social studies teacher and one of the students shared stories about their relatives from that era, and Australian-themed biscuits were baked at school to serve to community guests for morning tea. The day concluded with a Remembrance Day ceremony with much pomp and circumstance as students immersed themselves in the spirit of the era.

Project-based approach

A project-based approach to integration focuses on a designated task, often technology-based, that requires knowledge and skills from more than one subject area for its completion. Integration in this form is driven by a concluding event requiring the application and assembly of an array of knowledge and skills that come from different subjects. Unlike the thematic approach, where subjects tend to remain separate but are complementary to the theme, the connections between the knowledge and skills required to complete the project are more visible, so the subject boundaries become blurred. This is an interdisciplinary approach where the subjects are interconnected beyond a theme or issue, and where the connections are explicitly made and understood by the students. Often, project-based approaches are organized around the technology process of design, make and appraise, with links particularly to science, mathematics, engineering and materials. However, projects may also centre on other fields, such as food, the arts, social studies, health, English and other languages. In one of our Stage One case studies, at Southern High School, Year 9 students were given a design brief to build a model bridge in their technology and enterprise class. This project required knowledge from science and mathematics, as well as principles of engineering, aesthetics in design and being able to allocate time to complete the bridge on schedule. Although only one teacher was involved in teaching the class, care was taken to help students to see the links between the separate knowledge and skills needed in creating a model bridge. More about the bridge-building project is described in Chapter 5. We illustrate the project-based approach in this chapter using Eagleton Senior High School, another of our major Stage One case studies.

Eagleton Senior High School

Eagleton Senior High School was located in a well-established suburban area and had an academic extension class in each of Years 8, 9 and 10, in which the focus was on mathematics, science and technology. The technology teacher, who was also the coordinator of the academic extension programme, developed a number of technology projects that required science and mathematics knowledge in order for students to complete the project. He approached the science and mathematics teachers to see if ways could be found to offer a more integrated programme to the Year 9 class. At around this time, some funding enabled the refurbishment of an old industrial arts centre and this provided a classroom adjacent to a workshop where students could work on their projects and have some of their lessons. This facility acted as a catalyst to enthuse teachers about the possibility of an integrated programme.

Development of the project-based programme

Over a period of time, the science, mathematics and technology teachers documented what they were teaching in Year 9 and found there were significant overlaps. They spent two professional development days discussing the provision of a joint curriculum in which the final outcome would be the completion of a technology-driven project. Although the students attended separate classes for each of the three subjects, the teachers planned to synchronize their teaching so that the necessary knowledge and skills were provided at the right time to enable the students to complete their project using the knowledge and skills from all three subject areas.

The Year 9 students were given a brief to design and build a solar-powered boat that would out-perform other students' vessels. Students worked in pairs, and over a period of one term, teachers of science, mathematics and technology each taught the class the concepts from their subject area that were required for students to make decisions about building their boat. Important input from science included Archimedes' Principle, electrical circuits, current, resistance, Ohm's Law, power, solar energy and solar panels. In mathematics, the topics included indices, efficiency, critical pathways, graphs, solving equations and factorization. Hull shapes, propulsion methods, properties of relevant materials and construction techniques were central to the classes in technology. A specific example of the coming together of knowledge from the three subject areas is illustrated by the need for students to prepare a circuit to connect the solar cells to a motor from their science lessons; from mathematics, to understand what angle to attach the solar cells that would maximize power; and from technology, to design and make a hull so that the boat would not only float but be able to move with its load. On the culminating testing day, students were able to demonstrate whether or not their boat met the criteria stated in the design brief.

Outcomes of the project-based programme

Students became very involved in their solar boat project and, with the inherent element of competition, worked hard to achieve a working model. An important outcome noted by the teachers was the development of team building and learning about time management. Students were able to be creative and try out designs in an atmosphere that encouraged risk taking. They also got ideas from each other and from people beyond the classroom, and the application of some of the mathematics and science concepts gave students a better understanding of how things worked. Teachers also commented on students' willingness to write about their work, and each group made a video recording of their project as it developed, which provided an additional record to assist in assessment.

Cross-curricular approach

A cross-curricular approach to integration is based on major, overarching skills or habits, such as literacy, numeracy, environmental responsibility or the use of ICT, or perhaps on broad social skills, such as collaboration and cooperation. While this approach has some commonalities with a thematic approach, it differs in that it is more fundamentally embedded across the curriculum. Integration can occur because these skills are the focus of more than one subject at the same time. A cross-curricular issue will generally serve as a lead motive or *leitmotif* for teaching and learning. For example, at Hedgerow Primary School, one of our minor case studies in Stage One, technology and enterprise was used as an integrating subject across the curriculum. A range of ways was used to incorporate technology skills, including both the design and enterprise aspects as well as ICT, into social studies, art and science. Topics in mathematics and literacy were used to assist students to learn about the nature of enterprise. This approach to integration was interdisciplinary, in that there was some blurring of subject boundaries, particularly those of technology. An even more intense blurring of boundaries was achieved at Seaview Community School, our Stage One case study exemplar for a cross-curricular approach.

Seaview Community School

Seaview Community School was a small, geographically isolated school catering for students from Kindergarten to Year 10. Apart from the two children of the principal and his wife, also a teacher at the school, English was a second or third language for all students and their parents. Because of the non-English speaking background, and because all teaching is in English, a main focus of schooling in this region is the development of literacy. Seaview also has relatively high absenteeism, so many children lack continuity in their schooling, making it difficult for teachers to plan and carry out teaching sequences of more than a few days. The principal endeavoured to involve the school community as much as possible in school matters, both to encourage attendance and also to increase the relevance of what happened at school by involving it in what was happening in the community.

Development of the cross-curricular programme

The school's development plan was built around the community's expressed desire that the school should teach students to read, write and speak 'good English'. Consequently, teachers used literacy as a focus in every subject area, encouraging children to express themselves and communicate about their work in different ways. There were only three classes at Seaview, the youngest comprising children up to Year 3, an upper primary class of Years 4 to 7 and a high-school class of the Years 8 to 10 students, who tended to have a curriculum in which school subjects were more recognizable. The community is small and all teachers knew every child, which facilitated closeness between the school and community. It also meant that the four teachers, who all lived in the school grounds, had easy and frequent communication, so they were able to fit in with each other and change direction quickly if there were changes in the community that necessitated a response from the school.

Each of the three classes had its own integrated programme, centred around literacy. Because of students' non-English speaking background, all subjects have a large number of new words, and this is complicated by many words which do not have equivalent words in the home language. In art and science, for example, there are no equivalent words for 'colour' or 'space' or 'gravity'. Consequently, vocabulary building was an important part of every subject, as was helping students to structure sentences to write about what they have done. Every opportunity was taken to give students practice in reading, writing and speaking English.

One integrating programme that cut across the whole school was horticulture. The school had a large garden area that was continuously planted with various fruits and vegetables, with the concomitant harvesting, digging, fertilizing, mulching and replanting. The principal had a long-term plan to create a permaculture garden that he hoped would encourage the local community to grow their own fresh fruit and vegetables, which otherwise had to be trucked into the community. He considered the horticultural programme as meaningful, enjoyable and allowing maximum participation from the students. Further, it was able to be carried on by the students on their own, without needing the teacher, hence developing student independence. Most importantly, the garden introduced a great variety of activities in science, technology, social studies and mathematics, as well as providing opportunities to learn useful language and find ways to talk and write about it. Because the garden was a permanent asset, even though it was continually changing, students who missed considerable schooling could easily re-establish their connection with it on their return to school.

Outcomes of the cross-curricular programme

The cross-curricular integrated programme was central to the working of the school. The focus on literacy supported the students who had intermittent attendance, whose language and other skills deteriorated during their absence and had to be refreshed on their return to school. In particular, the horticultural programme created a sense of continuity for these transient students. It also supported the teachers in their focus on literacy, because all classes had their turn in the garden with various tasks to do. At Seaview all subjects naturally seemed to become integrated, because literacy was such a strong focus in the school. This was the most transdisciplinary curriculum we discovered in our research programme. Various concepts from all school subjects became implicit in everyday contexts that were meaningful to students and subject boundaries became irrelevant, except in some parts of the high-school class curriculum.

School-specialized approach

Under this approach to integration, a school adopts a specialized, long-term curriculum focus, such as aviation, performing arts or marine studies. Sometimes the specialization has a careers focus, such as aviation, and while this curriculum focus may have its own subject offerings, a school-specialized approach to integration means that this focus is embedded in the whole school curriculum. Other subject areas will contribute some topics that have explicit links to the specific specialization. There is frequently school-wide recognition of the specialization through activities or open days. Because the specialization permeates the staffing and infrastructure of the school, this approach does not rely for its survival on the enthusiasm and interest of individual teachers, but tends to be long term. Only one of the schools in our integration research took a school-specialized approach to integration. This occurred through the development of a marine studies programme in Oceanside High School, one of the minor case studies from Stage One.

Oceanside High School

Oceanside was a large metropolitan school located close to the shipping harbour, but also close to beaches fringed by reefs. The city overall has a strong beach culture with the ocean a major source of activity, both for industry and recreation. Over a long period, teachers at Oceanside have taken advantage of the school's location and developed a marine studies programme. The programme was designed to be a component of the usual subject curricula so that all students would be able to learn about something that was central to their life outside of school, with both local and global connections.

Development of the school-specialized programme

Rather than create a new, separate subject called marine studies, the school-specialized approach occurred through the integration of aspects of marine studies into a number of regular school subjects. An important factor in the development of the marine studies programme was the writing of a textbook by one of the teachers who was expert in the field. The textbook was used by all students in Years 8, 9 and 10. The teacher explained how he lobbied the teachers in the other subject areas to take on a part of the marine studies programme. As most of the students were able and enthusiastic, he was able to convince teachers that relevant aspects of the subject were worth incorporating into the teaching of their own subject.

Each of the subjects of science, technology and enterprise, social studies, and health and physical education taught one specified unit of marine studies to each year level in each academic year. For example, the Year 8 students studied weather and oceans in social studies; dangerous creatures, properties of seawater, pests and seabirds in science; boating in technology and enterprise; and water safety and snorkelling in physical education. The Year 9 marine studies topics included coastlines, sea pollution and shipwrecks in social studies; waves, currents, tides and seawater quality in science; fishing, fisheries and food from the sea in technology; and marine first aid in physical education.

Outcomes of the school-specialized programme

The marine studies programme has continued at Oceanside for over two decades because both teachers and students can see the connection to students' lives, and often to the occupations of family members. Most subject areas now have a section of their curriculum devoted to aspects of marine studies, including weather, currents and climate, human use of the ocean, marine ecology, water sports and so on. Some teachers, particularly when new to the school, may lack confidence because marine studies is not in their formal training, but they usually persist with it. In this they are assisted by the textbook written to support the programme. Teachers in English and mathematics also have taken advantage of the programme to include relevant aspects in their own teaching, so, overall, the school continues its marine studies focus.

Community-focused approach

A community-focused approach to integration involves a curriculum that reaches out beyond the school by investigating, in depth, some issue of significance in the community. School subjects are carefully aligned to bear on the issue, to understand it and to find and review potential solutions. Community-based approaches are similar to project-based approaches, in that they draw from the relevant disciplines the content and skills needed to understand or 'solve' some local problem or issue. In this way, the approach could be described as interdisciplinary, but it also has the potential to be more transdisciplinary, because it originates from a real-life community problem that provides a compelling context for making meaning from the issue itself, rather than drawing from within one discipline or another. Ideally, a community-based approach to integration goes beyond a theoretical consideration of a problem, involving also some individual or concerted action on the part of students, such as tree planting or writing letters to the local media.

One of our Stage Three case studies, Kentish Middle School, took the problem of nutrification in the local lake and investigated how the lake was used, monitored water quality, investigated the effects of housing projects, disposal of waste and adjacent parkland maintenance to prepare and argue for a management plan for the lake's future. This involved considerable blurring of boundaries across the subject areas because the integrated curriculum focused on the health of the lake, and also on the development of citizenship among the students, whose interests often led the direction of the studies. More about this case study appears in later chapters. In this chapter we use as our exemplar a different case study, also from Stage Three, where Chelsea Primary School and a wild life centre worked together to educate the local community about an ecological issue.

Chelsea Primary School

A partnership between the wild life centre at a local lake and Chelsea Primary School developed with the assistance of a small government grant to promote school and community interaction. The partnership was initiated by the manager of the wild life centre in response to concern for the sustainability of the lake's ecosystem. As the number of lakeside dwellings has increased, the venomous tiger snakes whose home is around the lake have ventured more often into residential properties, causing anxiety among local residents. The killing of many snakes had begun to create an ecological imbalance between the snakes and the frogs at the lake, which were the snakes' main food source. Chelsea is a small, independent primary school situated near the lake and many children from the local area attend the school. The partnership aimed to educate the children about this environmental issue and, through them, to promote their parents' and the community's awareness of the ecological significance of tiger snakes, and safety matters regarding the snakes, so that people and snakes could co-exist more comfortably.

Development of the community-based programme

Teachers from Chelsea and the centre manager collaborated on the development of a programme for the students in the two upper primary classes (mixed Years 4 to 7) in the school. Part of the programme was held at the centre and included guest herpetologists, who brought various reptiles for children to handle and tiger snakes (to look at, but not to be handled), as well as various student activities, such as learning and practising safety first in the case of snake bite, designing safety charts and interpretative signage for the lake. At school, students prepared a survey for community members, parents and friends to ascertain their attitudes towards and knowledge about snakes, collected and analysed the survey data, learned about food chains and species interdependence, and prepared presentations for a culminating community night. The extended school community was invited to this special event where students reported the findings from their research and the results of their activities.

The integrated programme was built around the values of social, civic and environmental responsibility, and seven of the eight discipline learning areas mandated in the state school curriculum. These areas were able to be addressed as part of the activities undertaken by the students both at the wild life centre and in their school classrooms. Outcomes in these learning areas were addressed as outlined below.

- Social Studies: Active citizenship through participation in survey data collection and presentation at the community night, contributing to a snake-safe neighbourhood.
- Science: Life and living through learning about organisms, the environment, food chains and food webs.
- The Arts: Dramatic role plays (presented at the community night), posters, badges, dioramas, computer graphics.
- English: Script writing and verbal presentations at the community night.
- Technology: Developing web-searching skills, preparing power-point presentations for the community night, building a model food pyramid.

- Mathematics: Collating and computing the survey data, developing graphs.
- Health and Physical Education: Learning and demonstrating first aid, learning about the difference between venomous and poisonous snakes, learning precautions to take when bush walking.

Although teachers kept the objectives of the various subject areas in the curriculum firmly in mind, the way the subjects were brought to bear can be described as transdisciplinary. In the students' view, the focus was the issue, not the school subjects, thus dissolving the boundaries between them. Students had considerable choice in what they chose to do for the community night, a role play, a poster, a presentation about their survey, for example, so there was considerable focus on allowing them to follow their interests. Further, the community-based approach enabled students to move out into the community, allowing the students to see the connectedness between what happened within the school doors and the world outside of school.

Outcomes of the community-based programme

Our research indicated that both the students' and the community's awareness of the ecology of the wetlands and the habitat of the tiger snakes was increased. For example, a key issue learned was that the behaviour of tiger snakes when confronted is defensive rather than aggressive. The wild life centre manager believed the centre benefited from the experience through heightened community awareness about tiger snakes (and indeed the centre's own programmes, which were mainly about bird life on the wetland). Lessons on safety measures and how to deal appropriately with tiger snakes were designed to reduce community anxiety regarding the snakes and, hopefully, result in a decreased snake mortality rate.

Chelsea students and their teachers benefited through an integrated programme in which students worked directly with a community partner on a recognized, real life problem. Students were trained in safety procedures and were able to demonstrate the first aid for snakebites. Community attitudes were surveyed, and students presented information regarding tiger snakes to the community group in the very successful community night which concluded the programme.

A broader perspective on integration

In this chapter, we have considered a variety of efforts to integrate curricula and revealed many different approaches to curriculum that were described by their innovators as integrated. We found that this diversity was at odds with descriptions in the literature that depict curriculum integration as having a distinct and separate structure compared with traditional discipline-based subject approaches to curriculum. Such a view suggests that a solution to understanding curriculum integration is to envisage a continuum with a discipline-based paradigm situated at one end and an integrated paradigm situated at the other end of the continuum. As we discussed earlier, some authors have proposed a curriculum structure based on this model, with different 'degrees' of integration at different points along the continuum, moving gradually into higher degrees of integration as more connections are made between subjects. The terms multidisciplinary, interdisciplinary and transdisciplinary are derived from this approach, and although teachers tend not to use these terms they can be useful, particularly in assisting description of one programme in comparison with another.

However, we have two concerns with the continuum-based means of describing integrated curricula. Our first concern is that the two-paradigm divide assumes a particular view of knowledge itself, where integrated knowledge is said to stand separately from other discipline-based forms of knowledge. Our view is that curriculum integration embraces many forms, as we have seen, and the knowledge that students gain, or the meaning they make from their learning experiences, is affected by the ease with which they can make connections between the various concepts they are learning about and the activities that provide the relevant reference framework, or context, that allows them to make these connections. We suggest that the nature of knowledge and how students learn about it is quite critical to its subsequent value to students. We take up this argument in Chapter 5.

Our second concern is that a continuum view of integrated curricula presupposes an integration hierarchy, underpinned by the implication that some kinds of integration are better than others, and where teachers progress from 'lesser' to more 'superior' forms of integration that may be observed and measured. The discussion of the case studies in the six, somewhat overlapping, approaches to curriculum integration we have described in this chapter has shown that how teachers respond to integration is not readily categorized as better or worse than another approach. Teachers try to do what is best for their students in the context of the school. In every case, teachers felt that they had achieved a positive difference, even though there were often great difficulties to overcome in implementing their programme. In the next chapter, we examine some of these implementation issues by looking at how schools and curriculum can be organized to support integrated practices.

3 Implementing curriculum integration
School and curriculum structures

In his classic study of school curricula, Basil Bernstein (1971, 2000) used the notions of classification and framing to generalize about the European (particularly British) approach to secondary schooling. He stated that some subjects, such as physics and chemistry, are strongly classified and strongly framed (that is, there are clear boundaries between subjects, and clear understandings on the part of teachers and students about what should or should not be taught). Other, more integrated, subjects, such as environmental, media or global studies, are weakly classified and weakly framed (that is, the boundaries between subjects are unclear, and there is ambiguity about what should or should not be taught). Bernstein's ideas explain much about why integrated programmes often struggle to establish their identity in a school system that is generally rigid, differentiating, hierarchical and highly resistant to change.

Essentially, the weakly framed and classified character of integrated curricula is at odds with the rigid nature of what Tylack and Tobin (1994) called 'the grammar of schooling'. Grammar underpins the culture of schools and is reinforced by the customs, rituals, ceremonies and artefacts of everyday school life (Deal and Kennedy, 1982). Once established, the grammar of schooling is difficult to change. Many factors contribute to the strength and persistence of the grammar of secondary schools, including teacher recruitment and identity, subject histories, assessment structures, department politics, subject status, student futures, and an overcrowded and content-laden curriculum (Hargreaves et al., 1996). Of particular importance to the institutional context, according to Hall and Kidman (2004), is the ethos towards teaching and learning communicated by the individual departments or academic units within the institution. A crucial finding from Wood, Lawrenz, Huffman and Schultz (2006) was that students, teachers and principals differ in their perceptions of school context. Further, the ways in which teachers talked about curriculum, instruction and assessment varied more within a particular school than across schools. This finding challenges the notion of the secondary school as a single culture; rather, it exists as a series of departmental subcultures, each with particular subject interests.

In their study of the factors influencing the success or failure of integrated programmes, Pang and Good (2000) distinguished between contextual variables, such as administrative policies, curriculum and testing constraints, school traditions, and teacher variables, such as subject matter knowledge, pedagogical content knowledge and beliefs, as well as their instructional practices. With respect to contextual variables, our own research (Venville *et al.*, 2008) showed a strong relationship between educational context and the way that an integrated, community-based project about the environment was implemented (see Chapter 4). Within the context of Brampton High School, a traditional secondary school, we found that the form of curriculum integration implemented was quite different to that implemented in Kentish Middle School, a purpose-built Years 6 to 9 school with a similar demographic. The contextual factors included school organization, classroom structure, timetable, teacher qualifications, collaborative planning time and approach to assessment.

In terms of teacher variables, it is difficult to overstate the importance of content and pedagogical content knowledge. Integrated curricula often require teachers to teach out of field, impacting both their confidence and ability to teach (Kruse and Roehrig, 2005). In an example from science, Levinson (2001) found that it is challenging for teachers to address the ethics and controversies of contemporary local and global science issues. He concluded that few teachers, whatever their speciality, can handle these areas with much confidence or expertise. This is not due to any inadequacy on their part, but to the complexity of the issues. This scenario is often compounded with beginning teachers, who have limited pedagogical knowledge and experience in managing classroom activities. Some of these issues can be addressed through collaboration among teachers from different disciplines (Venville, Wallace, Rennie and Malone, 2000), but it is not easy. All too often, we find teachers reverting to the comfortable patterns of practice associated with their own subject speciality.

Teachers are also often torn between what might be termed epistemological idealism and institutional pragmatism with regard to curriculum integration. Kain (1996) observed that many teachers articulated their ideals about the possibilities of a more holistic view of knowledge and an integrated curriculum, but they routinely saw the limits of this view through the realities of the classrooms and the institutions within which they worked. While teachers may be empowered to make decisions about the delivery of the curriculum, they cannot escape the grips of institutional constraints and this, in turn, limits their decision making within their own classroom (Kain, 1996).

A further tension is to be found in the views of parents and other curriculum stakeholders. Brantlinger and Majd-Jabbari (1998) found that while college-educated, middle-class parents espoused support for open, integrated, multicultural, student-centred education, their narratives revealed a preference for conservative practice. They favoured factual, tightly-sequenced, subject-area-bound, Western-oriented curricula because, the authors suggest, generations of their class had relatively uncontested success within this traditional approach to curriculum. An integrated curriculum is inconsistent with the expectation in many places that the school curriculum should be academically oriented, emphasizing written work and individual study, and focused on examinable concepts and ideas (Kaplan, 1997).

To summarize, implementing and sustaining an integrated approach to the school curriculum presents a particular set of challenges for teachers, administrators and others concerned with curriculum reform. The challenges can be largely explained by an underlying tension between a curriculum approach, which by its very nature is flexible, multidisciplinary and democratic, and a schooling context (including school organization, timetables, assessment practices, teacher preparation and identity, and parental expectations), which is rigid, disciplinary and hierarchical. Changing the context of schooling – what Hall and Kidman (2004) referred to as the manner in which the institution provides the 'strategic direction, policies, conditions and many of the rules that govern the way that teaching, learning and assessment take place' (p. 334) – appears to be a key factor in the introduction of integrated practices. While we do have some good examples of successful programmes described in the literature (e.g., Lingard, Ladwig, Luke, Mills, Hayes and Gore, 2001), we also know that reform efforts are patchy and difficult to sustain over time, with participants often reverting to traditional structures and practices when energy flags, support lessens and things get difficult.

In this chapter, we examine the topic of implementation in two ways. First, we draw from our work with schools over 15 years to build some case knowledge about the kinds of school structures and key programme characteristics that appear to support curriculum integration. Second, we look at the various ends-in-view or interests of curriculum integration to propose a practical integrated planning and teaching framework based on what we call a Worldly Perspective on curriculum.

School structures

In this section, we draw on data from a number of our case study schools to identify those conditions that are likely to maintain and sustain integrated practice over the long term. A summary of these conditions is presented in Table 3.1. Overall, we found that the enabling conditions for integration fell under four broad categories: shared purpose, collegial relations, norms of improvement and structure. Shared purpose refers to shared ideas about the purposeful educational direction of the school and, in the schools described, included such things as administrative and community support. Collegial relations refers to the ways in which mutual sharing, assistance and joint effort among teachers was valued and honoured in the school, exemplified by how the teaching teams worked together. Norms of improvement refers to the way in which teachers were seeking to improve their practices, exemplified by

Table 3.1 Summary of enabling and inhibiting conditions

School	Enabling conditions	Inhibiting conditions
Beachville Public School	• planning time • committed teachers • collective vision	• teacher workload
Eagleton Senior High School	• teaching teams • collective vision • dedicated teaching space • meeting time • flexible timetable	• teacher workload • planning time
Florabunda District High School	• collective vision • dedicated teaching space • planning time • outcomes approach	• staff turnover • community wariness
Greenbelt Community College	• teaching teams • flexible timetable • administrative support • collective vision	• teacher workload • community wariness • teaching out of field • teaching materials
Greenwich Public School	• dedicated teaching space • flexible timetable	• teacher workload
Hillsdale Christian School	• administrative support • planning time • committed teachers	• teaching materials • teaching out of field • time
Mossburn School	• administrative support • planning time • dedicated teaching space	• staff turnover
Oceanside High School	• marine studies coordinator • administrative support • teaching resources • committed teachers	• coordinator dependent • communication time • timetable restrictions
Redwood Senior High School	• planning time • committed teachers • team approach	• staff turnover • teaching out of field • perception of forced or contrived integration • planning time
Rinkview Public School	• teaching teams • collective vision • dedicated teaching space • meeting time • flexible timetable	• teacher workload • planning time • content knowledge • crowded curriculum
Riverview Ladies College	• flexible timetable • dedicated teaching space • committed teachers • team approach • planning time	• finding committed middle-school teachers

Continued

Table 3.1 Cont'd

School	Enabling conditions	Inhibiting conditions
Sandbanks Community High School	• administrative support • teaching teams • collective vision • flexible timetable	• teaching out of field • teacher workload
Seaview Community School	• administrative support • flexible structures • small school size • community support	• staff turnover • transient student population

teacher commitment. The fourth category, structure, refers to those organizational arrangements and policies that worked in support of the other three conditions.

Inhibiting conditions, in many ways, matched but also opposed the enabling conditions. Factors working against shared purpose, for example, included community wariness that integrated teaching approaches might be 'watering down' the curriculum, teachers with different disciplinary traditions, and the arrival of new staff with different ideas. Working against sound collegial relations was the problem of teachers having to teach out of field, a perception by some teachers that integration was being forced upon them, and high rates of staff (and student) turnover. Heavy teacher workloads worked against norms of improvement, and structural problems identified included a lack of planning time, timetabling restrictions and a lack of sound teaching resources to support integrated practices.

In this chapter, we focus on those common (mainly structural) key programme characteristics or attributes that appear to present across most of the schools we have studied. The six characteristics are small and stable learning environments, leadership, team activities linked to the classroom, in-school planning time, flexible timetable and community links.

Small and stable learning environments for teachers and students

One of the most striking characteristics of the integrated programmes we have observed is that the teachers and students were members of small and stable learning environments. Sometimes called teams or learning communities, small learning environments typically involved a small interdisciplinary team of teachers (usually four or less) with shared responsibility for a small (usually less than 90) group of students. Such configurations were observed at most of the schools in our studies. At Eagleton Senior High School, for example, the science, mathematics and technology teachers collaborated on a year-long integrated programme for approximately 30 Year 9 students. In a series of project-based units the students were asked to design and produce vehicles such as a solar-powered boat and a hill-climbing car. The students were taught separate discipline-related material by their subject teachers and provided with 'common' time to work in groups of two or three to design, make and evaluate their models. At Rinkview Public School, the two Year 8 teachers combined their classes to create a pod of 50 students for a 6-week integrated unit called 'Making and Marketing a Toy'. The students worked in groups of four, with the teachers cooperating to teach the requisite skills in mathematics, science, technology, business studies, etc., and to monitor the construction and marketing of the toy. The teachers at Kentish Middle School implemented their 10-week integrated project in a learning community of 120 students (five classes). The project examined water quality (nutrification) in a local recreational lake, with the five teachers working collaboratively to plan and implement the project.

An additional key factor was stability – of programmes, of staff and of relationships. Stable programmes were those where teaming practices had been in place over a number of years (notably Greenbelt, Sandbanks and Riverview); stable staff meant that programmes retained key personnel; and stable relationships were assisted when teaching teams followed groups of students from one year to the next (a feature of most of the middle-school programmes we studied). Small and stable learning environments led to a tight reciprocity of teaching and learning. At Sandbanks, for example, the students and teachers in Years 8 to 10 were organized into interdisciplinary learning teams with 4–5 teachers responsible for approximately 100 students. One teacher commented on the advantage of this approach:

> If [the students] know that we are talking among each other and we are making sure that we are keeping up with the kids and what we are doing in each subject, well they can't slack off in one subject and keep up on the other. It's a two way street.
>
> (Venville *et al.*, 1999a, p. 33)

Finally, we note that small and stable learning environments were sometimes located in large schools, where students and teachers belonged to small learning sub-communities situated within larger school environments. At Rinkview, for example, the learning community consisted of the two Year 8 teachers and their combined classes, and at Beachville the 23 Year 9 applied students shared a common group of teachers. These sub-communities provided safe and stable places for students to learn and interact with peers and teachers, separate from, but connected to, the wider school.

Leadership

Leadership is often cited as an important precondition for curriculum reform. This was also the case in the schools in our studies, where leadership was evident in a variety of forms. In almost every case, participants mentioned the importance of a supportive administration. For example, at Sandbanks, one teacher said 'as far as the administration is concerned, they are right behind us because whatever we want to try, we have their support' (Venville *et al.*, 1999a, p. 33). We took this to mean a number of things, ranging from the hands-on transformative leadership of the principal (as we observed in Greenbelt, Sandbanks and Seaview) to enabling support in the form of resource provision and encouragement. At Seaview, for example, the principal, Mr Lanyon, worked collaboratively with his staff to embed the school's emphasis on language skills into the school purpose statement and to integrate language across all aspects of the school curriculum. At Mossburn, the lead teacher reported that

> The principal was very much behind us all the way. Like he was very much 'Great, great, great, yes. How's it going?' ... We had a science show at the end of it and the parents were invited to come and so was the principal and they were the judges as well.

A further form of leadership involved programme coordination, and many of our case study schools saw teachers in this role. Oceanside, for example, appointed a dedicated coordinator to provide leadership and resource support for the school's marine studies specialization, and Redwood and Sandbanks appointed programme leaders to each learning team. Perhaps the most pervasive form was the kind of distributed or shared leadership exercised across teaching teams. In the Kentish example, while two of the teachers (Mr Keane and Ms Price) were the driving force behind the water quality project, other teachers took the lead at different times. Ms Price commented that

> In maths, we did a lot of graphing, measurement, lots of measurement. ... So the way we worked, Amanda, who developed the maths programme, covered that in maths. So we were already thinking at the beginning, when is the mathematical thinking coming in this topic. So when we needed to apply a maths concept in science or S and E [Society and Environment], we asked her to do it in maths. It's a bit like circular planning. The whole thing spirals on itself.
>
> (Venville *et al.*, 2008, p. 870)

At Hillsdale, while the original suggestion for an integrated project came from the mathematics teacher, the idea was soon taken up by his social studies colleague, who proposed a joint project on global North–South inequities. This kind of distributed leadership was evident in most of the schools we observed. It was evident in the way that people referred to the commitment and enthusiasm of their colleagues, and in the way that team members shared responsibility and contributed jointly to the development and implementation of ideas. In the words of one of the teachers from Sandbanks,

There's a backup of three other teachers who are having the same thoughts, the same ideas. ... They've also had a chance to iron out the mistakes you've made, and you can look at theirs and give them a different perspective on what they're doing. ... It makes everything more ... holistic.

Team activities linked to the classroom

We found that teacher team activities were strongly connected to classroom instructional practices. Such activities included coordinating curriculum, classroom-level integration and interdisciplinary practices. At Greenbelt, for example, where the Year 7, 8 and 9 teachers worked collaboratively in learning teams to design, implement and assess interdisciplinary modules, team members 'share[d] 80 to 90 percent of their curriculum materials with each other' (Venville *et al.*, 1999a, p. 12). Teachers referred specifically to team time being used to develop themes, identify links across learning areas, develop common outcomes, coordinate assessments, organize to teach interrelated concepts and discuss how to embed constructivist pedagogical strategies. As one teacher from Florabunda (where the curriculum in Years 8–10 was organized around common themes) described it, '[We would get together to talk about] how everyone was going, how the timing was going, slot in with other classes, and then make adjustments to your part of the programme'.

At Beachville, for example, the Year 9 science (Ms Wade) and geography (Mr Norris) teachers taught their respective energy units in parallel. Together they planned the content of the two subjects, identified specific cross-subject links, and made regular visits to each other's classrooms. Ms Wade explained,

> I think that probably to the largest effect [of our joint activities] was the fact that Mr Norris and I were both conscious of being on top of our game and being on top of the kids and on top of what are they going to learn next, what things do I have to cover.

Here, and in many of our case study schools, the teachers' classroom-focused team activities served to build teaching capacity, but also to model cooperative learning to students. At Eagleton, for example, the technology, science and mathematics teachers collaboratively planned and taught an integrated programme based on technology-driven project work. The teachers frequently commented on how they learned from each other and how their learning and joint problem-solving provided a model for their students.

In-school planning time

The call for quality planning time was a common refrain among the case study teachers. In the words of Mr Norris, the geography teacher at Beachville,

I mean planning, proper planning of it … it's hard to do on the fly, over the year, with sports that are running and this and that. I mean, we're all involved in so much outside of school, it's hard to figure out a schedule when we can all meet.

The availability of dedicated in-school planning time was a feature of several schools in our study. At Greenbelt, for example, planning time was prioritized by the deputy principal 'as an essential prerequisite for the development of an integrated curriculum' (Venville *et al.*, 1999a, p. 12). At Florabunda, three half-hour, shared planning sessions were incorporated into the timetable and a separate staff planning area established. One teacher made the following statement:

I believe that one of the most powerful things we have been able to do certainly with the secondary teachers and now with the junior primary teachers is to give them collaborative planning time. The wonderful thing that we did … was … a secondary planning area and it was just one big open space and we actually had all the teachers around the room and the whole notion was that they would be there together, they would be talking and meeting and planning together and it actually did happen and it was a very exciting year.

(Venville *et al.*, 1999a, p. 18)

At Riverview, the five Year 8 teachers worked as a team to develop and teach a series of integrated topics (on the environment, for example) incorporating aspects of all learning areas. Weekly professional development sessions were scheduled for teachers to examine links between learning areas and to develop common themes. In all the cases we studied, in-school planning time (and often a dedicated space) served to provide teachers with the resources to collaborate and innovate, and signalled to all that such work is important and central.

Flexible timetable

Another common feature of the case study schools was the enabling role of a flexible timetable. In those schools where teaming was a feature, the central timetable established only the broad structure, while pedagogical decisions about student grouping, teaching time and space allocation were typically devolved to the teaching team. As one teacher at Sandbanks said,

we can shuffle it around, I will take science at this time if I can put my kids into maths and swap it around like that. It's just negotiating. … It is really good not to be stuck to a timetable.

(Venville *et al.*, 1999a, p. 34)

What the flexible models had in common was the goal of lengthening blocks of learning time and reducing the number of transitions students needed to make between teachers, classes, subjects and experiences. One advantage was that teachers could work with different groups of students at different times, depending on the needs of the students.

Three of the large schools (Greenbelt, Sandbanks and Riverview) used block timetabling across the entire middle school, so that learning teams could effectively operate as sub-schools. The dedicated academic extension programmes at Redwood and Eagleton were largely independent from the constraints of the larger school timetable. At Eagleton, for example, the integrated programme operated in a dedicated technology centre. The science and mathematics components were taught separately, with common teaching time for designing, making and appraising the technology projects. In the rural and primary schools that we studied (such as Seaview, Florabunda and Rinkview), the small size of the school allowed considerable scope for teachers to work together to integrate the curriculum.

Community links

The final characteristic of the integrated programmes described in our case studies is community links. Our observation is that this characteristic operates at two levels. The first level – the level of information – concerns the importance of bringing the local community 'onside' with school policy and practice. Teachers at Greenbelt, Sandbanks and Florabunda spoke specifically of the need to routinely inform the community about integrated teaching practices, and of the dangers of not doing so. As one teacher put it,

> Community perception is important, particularly when you are introducing an integrated programme that differs from the norm. Parents often find it different because it is so different from their own personal [school] experience and they having nothing to relate it to. We have worked hard to keep the community onside and to inform them about what we are doing.

Many of the programmes incorporated specific opportunities for parents and other community members to come to the school to observe and participate in classroom activities. For example, at Mossburn, parents were invited to view and judge the final doll's house projects. At Redwood, parents and other community members participated in ANZAC Day[1], as the culminating activity for the integrated 'My Heritage' module.

At a second (and arguably more significant) level – the level of action – the teaching programme reached out to involve, and contribute to, the local community in a more 'integrated' fashion. This level of community linkage is illustrated by the integrated programmes at Brampton and Kentish, focusing on the study of midge (at Brampton) and water nutrients (at Kentish) in local lakes (Venville *et al.*, 2008). In each case, the projects were teamed with a local university, the local city council and the water authority. The projects addressed local as well as global issues, drew on local expertise, and reported results to the local community. In another example, at Seaview, a remote area school with an explicit cross-curricular focus on language (both the local indigenous language and English), the principal and students were endeavouring to involve the community in their horticulture programme. At Hillsdale, we offer another example of students informing themselves and considering ways of taking action on the topic of global North–South inequities. Over the course of our work on integration, we have come to view community links (particularly at the level of action) as a most important characteristic of integrated practice.

*   *   *   *

Our intention here has been to offer a few key programme attributes rather than an exhaustive list of all the factors likely to impact on programme success. The list is mainly structural and does not include other conditions such as norms of improvement and collegiality. In many respects, these attributes are similar to those identified in other empirical studies. For example, in a major study of Australian middle-school reform, Pendergast and colleagues (2005) found that teacher teaming, innovative leadership and connections between student learning and the outside world were important early structural features of most schools. In the US, a major review by Visher, Emanual and Teitelbaum (1999) highlighted the importance of small learning environments, flexible relevant scheduling and links to the outside community. Summarizing their findings from a decade of middle-grades research in the US, Flowers, Mertens and Mulhall (2003) emphasized several reform conditions, including small interdisciplinary teams, common planning time and teacher development linked to classroom practice. In a major Canadian study, Hargreaves, Earl, Moore and Manning (2001) found that middle schools worked best when they embraced relevant and integrated curricula, were configured in small flexible learning teams, and connected teacher development directly to classroom practice.

While the findings from these studies are closely aligned with our own, we caution against the tendency to see school curriculum reform in terms of identifying and implementing individual structural characteristics. While it is instructive to isolate certain key attributes, we propose that it is the *combination of characteristics* that matters. For example, leadership alone is unlikely to make a difference if teaching teams are unstable, and team activities are likely to be more effective when common planning time is provided. Another important finding is that schools exhibited these characteristics in different ways. The organization of small learning environments and flexible school days, for example, differed from team to team and from school to school. Finally, we caution that the six characteristics were not present in all of the integrated programmes we observed. Curriculum integration was supported in many ways, not always conforming to the six attributes described above.

Curriculum structures

In this section of the chapter, we shift our attention from the key structural characteristics supporting an integrated approach to the structures of an integrated curriculum. An integrated approach, it is argued, places the learner at one with nature; entwined and implicated in local and global conditions, large and small (Davis, Sumara and Luce-Kapler, 2000). Such curricula should focus on big curriculum ideas, based on problems or issues of personal and social significance in the 'real' world (Beane, 1996). These big curriculum ideas should form the organizing centre of the school curriculum, with other components linking or jigsawing into them. Under an integrated approach, students are provided with opportunities to engage with and make sense of those ideas in learning communities, to solve problems and, importantly, to act thoughtfully on their new understandings.

One way of conceptualizing the various ends-in-view or goals of integrated teaching is in terms of curriculum interests. The notion of interests draws heavily on the work of Habermas (1971), who distinguished between the interests of the empirical-analytic sciences, the hermeneutic-historical sciences and the critical sciences. These three sets of interests are often referred to as the *technical* interest, concerned with rule-like regularities; the *practical* interest, concerned with relating and communicating; and the *critical* interest, concerned with political action. Habermas also referred to two aspects of the practical interest, the personal (making personal meaning of situations) and the problem-solving (resolving practical problems).

Here we illustrate the different interests of curriculum integration by reference to two middle-school cases, one an illustration of community-focused integration and the second an example of the project-based form. The first case, described in more detail in Lloyd and Wallace (2004), involved a class of Year 9 middle-school students in a long-term study of fresh water ecology and the fresh water needs of South Australian residents. The second case, Eagleton, is described in detail in Venville *et al.* (2000). It involved middle-school students designing, constructing and evaluating the performance of a solar-powered boat.

Technical interest

The technical interest in curriculum integration refers to the need for students to come to a better understanding of the techniques, ideas and concepts behind the topic. It involves a serious engagement with the canons of knowledge in the various subjects, attending to the interest of knowing how the world works from various disciplinary standpoints.

In the fresh water ecology case, wetland management was a major focus. As Lloyd and Wallace (2004) explained, the middle-school students became involved in a scientific study of aspects of the nature of water, water quality (chemical and biological), types of micro- and macro-invertebrates, aquatic plant life and macro-fauna, and ecological aspects such as energy transfer. Students also examined the consequences of land clearing on water salinity, the effects of degrading riparian zones, the effects of altering food chains, the problems associated with introducing exotic species, and the effects human lifestyles can have on wetlands. Associated concepts included more global social phenomena such as the nature of human communities and political institutions, the economics of water supply and water conservation, and the technical requirements of preparing environmental impact statements.

In the solar-powered boat example, three Year 9 teachers collaborated to synchronize and integrate the content and teaching processes in the three learning areas of science, mathematics and technology. One of the components of the project required students to tabulate the current, voltage and power for several circuits for various solar cell combinations. As Venville *et al.* (2000) explained, during science, students were taught the concepts of current, voltage, resistance and power, and circuitry. They were asked to set up their circuits and test with a multi-meter the cells in series, in parallel and in combinations of both series and parallel. During mathematics, the students were taught how to read a sun chart for latitude 32°S (the latitude of the school located in Perth, Australia) so that they could work out where the sun would be at the appropriate time on the final testing day. In technology, the students were introduced to design and construction techniques, properties of materials and the importance of testing and evaluation.

While the nature of these examples may seem self-evident, the reality is that choosing the appropriate depth and breadth of technical treatment is not always easy. While science teachers, for example, may feel an obligation to teach the detailed physics, chemistry or ecology of water, these aspects may not always be essential for a good understanding of the broader topic of wetland management. Moreover, a science teacher's view of what is important technical knowledge is likely to be different from that of a social studies teacher or of a student. As Shulman and Sherin (2004) pointed out, the direct connection between the content taught and the bigger integrated idea is not always apparent, particularly at the beginning of a topic. Many questions remain. How much (and what kind of) technical knowledge? Who decides? How does this knowledge jigsaw into the larger curriculum idea?

Practical interest

The practical interest refers to the manner in which students make personal sense of the integrated topic at hand, how they solve problems and communicate their ideas. The emphasis here is on personal and communal sense making, finding the links between and across different discipline areas and with students' worlds, testing new ways of doing things, and working with others.

The water quality topic presented many possibilities for exploring the practical interest (Lloyd and Wallace, 2004). Students considered the past, present and possible future use of wetlands and rivers, including indigenous and European use. Water-management practices by local officials, the views of environmental advocates, and media and government reports were also examined. Students considered the global, societal, environmental and technological impacts of various water-management strategies. Futures wheels and cross-impact matrices were used to assist students to develop a personal and arguable rationale about water use in their local setting.

The practical interest was also evident in the solar-powered boat example, where students worked with peers to make links between technical knowledge and practical problem-solving situations. According to Venville *et al.* (2000), this practical interest was particularly evident at three critical decision points in the boat's construction, namely hull design, circuit design and solar cell orientation. In designing the hull, students employed scientific and technological principles to build a stable boat capable of carrying a load of solar panels and a motor, and being propelled at optimum speed. Students were also required to use their scientific understandings to test various series and parallel circuits to help them decide on a configuration to provide their motor with maximum power output. Drawing on their mathematics understandings, students also needed to decide on the most suitable mount for their solar panels so that the optimum angle to the sun could be achieved on the testing day.

In each of the above examples, there was ample evidence of discussion, sourcing alternatives, debate, disputation, justification and testing of ideas. The practical interest is also a place where the solutions and traditions offered by the technical interest are tested against one another. In the solar boat project, for example, students found that technical scientific and mathematical knowledge did not always offer easy solutions to the messy practical problem of boat design. Frequently, it was the methods of technology, with its practical traditions of design, make and appraise, that provided a way forward. This observation speaks to another challenge, that of bringing together subjects (and teachers) with different curricular traditions.

Critical interest

The critical interest involves questioning current practices, considering how those practices may be changed, and taking personal or political action to achieve changes in the status quo. The emphasis here is on examining the taken-for-granted, achieving consensus and finding a balance between personal, community and future generational needs.

This interest, according to Lloyd and Wallace (2004), is about shared decision making. In the water-quality example, students developed ideas about how they could make a difference and devised strategies and action plans for getting there. This was a shared and collective task based on an informed view of the issues they had studied. Actions included writing an article for a local newspaper, producing a display for the school library, and getting involved with a local action group or the school's 'Waterwatch' or 'Frogwatch' programmes. However, as Lloyd and Wallace (2004) pointed out, the extent of student involvement was not the greatest concern. Rather, the critical interest was about students contributing meaningfully and tangibly towards a better future for themselves and for others.

The critical interest is less evident in the solar-powered boat example. However, one could imagine a critical component involving students in discussions and actions around alternative energy sources, such as solar power, the emissions caused by diesel-powered boating and shipping, and other local and global energy issues. Alternatively, students could investigate and consider their own possible futures in science and technology, including careers in marine or electrical engineering, or some aspect of boating as a hobby.

In pursuing the critical interest, we are faced with the continuing problem of linking the interest with the big curriculum ideas. Some big ideas, particularly environmental ideas such as wetland management or social concerns such as ethnic conflict or abortion, have obvious critical components. Indeed, some commentators (for example, Wilson, 1998) argue that the curriculum should be largely guided by these big, global, critical issues facing humankind, including arms escalation, overpopulation, the greenhouse effect and endemic poverty. However, there is also strong justification for incorporating big ideas that lend themselves to a more technical or practical treatment. These ideas could be technological, as in the solar boat project, mathematical, historical, literary, artistic or otherwise. Some ideas are bigger than others, some more locally focused, others more global in nature, and some strategies for implementing those ideas are bolder than others. The choice of idea and strategy depends on the context, experience and the needs of the community of learners.

Planning for integration: Adopting a Worldly Perspective

In Chapter 2 we noted that curriculum integration is often described in the literature as having a different and separate structure to that of the traditional discipline-based approach to curriculum. We wrote of a strong temptation to postulate two paradigms, a discipline-based paradigm and an integrated paradigm, situated at either end of a continuum. We mentioned how some authors (e.g., Applebee *et al.*, 2007; Drake, 1998; Fogarty, 1991) proposed curriculum structures in just this way, with increasing 'degrees' of integration as one moves along the continuum from the discipline-based end to the integrated end. We pointed out our concerns with this approach: that the implicit hierarchy suggests that some forms of integration are 'better' than others, and that there are underlying assumptions about the nature of knowledge itself, that is, integrated knowledge is somehow separate from other discipline-based forms of knowledge. Instead, and as documented in Chapter 2, curricula described as integrated exist in many different forms in many different contexts.

In this book we argue for a Worldly Perspective on integration (Venville *et al.*, 2002). This perspective recognizes the legitimacy and importance of the different curriculum approaches and interests and their contributions to knowledge. We acknowledge, for example, that disciplinary or technical knowledge interests present powerful tools for representing and understanding the world and for solving practical and critical problems. But a Worldly Perspective also invites teachers and students to view the curriculum from whole to part, with big issues, concerns or interests becoming the organizing framework rather than serving as illustrations of disciplinary concepts. Such an organizing framework also enables the curriculum to demonstrate the connect-edness between local and global issues.

To illustrate the Worldly Perspective, we draw on the work of Lloyd and Wallace (2004) to propose an integrated teaching framework involving five intersecting elements:

- selecting the topic around a big curriculum idea;
- eliciting students' prior understandings;
- learning about the way the world works (the technical interest);
- making personal sense and solving practical problems (the practical interest); and
- acting thoughtfully to find harmony between personal, community and local as well as global future generational needs (the critical interest).

These five elements could form the basis for a sequential 'topic plan', but are more appropriately used as referents for curriculum planning. An elabora-tion of each element can be found in Table 3.2. The first element is the big idea itself. As we have illustrated in the several forms of integration described earlier, big ideas can range from overarching local and global themes, issues or projects, such as conflict, narrative, poverty, genetic engineering or Aboriginality, to important interconnecting links between subjects, such as computer or graphing skills, writing genres or critical thinking. Selection of big ideas will be guided by teachers' understandings of important issues, students' needs in terms of life-skills and interests, and important community issues, both local and global.

Eliciting students' prior knowledge is the second element. The focus here is to examine students' backgrounds, experiences and understandings with respect to the big ideas contained in the topic. This helps to identify and define the topic as perceived by the students. The aim is to acknowledge students' viewpoints, establish the topic as an important area of study and provide a foundation for topic planning. Various teaching strategies can be used to elicit students' prior understandings, including brainstorming, futures imaging, and stating and critiquing viewpoints.

The third to fifth elements of a Worldly Perspective involve attending to the various knowledge interests, the technical, the practical and the critical. As we have seen in the examples described above, the balance among these three will depend largely on the nature of the big idea or topic. Some ideas will lend themselves to a greater emphasis on the critical (for example, community-focused), others on the practical (for example, project-based), and so on. Generally speaking, however, the various interests should be seen as building blocks in integrated teaching and learning. First, students' opinions and understandings about the big ideas need to be informed by a solid foundation of technical knowledge; that is, knowledge about how the world works from various disciplinary standpoints. Second, students need to make sense of, and test out, new understandings by undertaking practical inquiry and problem-solving activities. Finally, students act on their new understandings by seeking ways of balancing personal, community and future needs. Each of the three interests is guided by the kinds of curriculum questions and teaching strategies proposed in Table 3.2.

Finally: Easing the tension

Integrated approaches to teaching and learning are beset by an underlying tension between the flexibility of the curriculum and the rigidity of the school structures within which the curriculum operates. In this chapter we offered some practical ways of easing this tension – by pointing to a series of enabling structural arrangements in the schools we have studied, and proposing an integrated planning and teaching framework based on what we call a Worldly Perspective on curriculum.

In the first instance, we are advocating school structures that are more flexible and more responsive to the needs of teachers and students. While conditions such as small and stable learning environments, active leadership, productive team activities, planning time, flexible timetables and links to the community are important, they do not provide the whole picture. Schools, like all institutions, are buffeted by the vagaries of a raft of external and internal pressures. The challenge for innovative schools, such as those described in this research, is to find embedded ways of *both* strengthening programmes *and* responding to these pressures. Resilient schools, those able to sustain innovative integrated programmes over the long term, manage to hold the enabling and inhibiting conditions in a kind of productive balance – shared against individual purposes, collegial against isolated practices, improvement against maintenance norms and enabling against inhibiting structures.

In the second instance, we are proposing a more balanced and more pragmatic approach to integrated curricula that recognizes the central contribution of disciplinary knowledge in integrated programmes. Our perspective on integration – a Worldly Perspective – is focused around interesting and significant ideas that promote wholeness and unity rather than separation and fragmentation. Importantly, a Worldly Perspective recognizes the legitimacy of the

Table 3.2 A teaching framework incorporating a Worldly Perspective on curriculum integration

Curriculum element	Curriculum focus	Curriculum questions	Forms of integration	Strategies
Big idea	Selecting the topic	What life skills do students need? What issues are of immediate concern to students? What are the big local/global issues?	All forms	Mapping existing curriculum documents, identifying community issues and current affairs, surveying students and parents
Prior knowledge	Eliciting students' prior understandings	What are students' backgrounds, experiences and understandings?	All forms	Brainstorming, elicitation, futures imaging, critiquing viewpoints
Technical interest	Learning about the way the world works	What essential technical knowledge will best prepare students?	All forms	Direct instruction, reading, field trips, laboratory activities
Practical interest	Making personal sense and solving practical problems	What kinds of (guided) inquiry will help students to make sense of the idea?	Potentially all forms, particularly project-based, thematic and cross-curricular	Guided inquiry, experimentation, problem solving, creative writing, model building
Critical interest	Acting thoughtfully	What kinds of actions are appropriate for this group of students?	Potentially all forms, particularly community-focused and school-specialized	Community projects, letter writing, debates, theme days

different knowledge interests and the need to find an appropriate balance among those interests. It also recognizes the connectedness between local and global issues. This kind of approach acknowledges the practicalities of curriculum change and the challenges faced by teachers as they are asked to do different things with the disciplines, learn new kinds of pedagogical content understandings and work with their colleagues in new ways.

This tension between context and curriculum is an uneasy and delicate one. For example, a number of the teachers in our case study schools highlighted the constant tussle between the forces for a more subject-discipline-based approach and the forces for a more integrated approach. Other teachers mentioned the battle to establish collaborative in-school planning time or the struggle to win community support. When this tension becomes less than productive, schools are more likely to revert to less integrated forms of teaching. The best we can hope for is to provide safe, stable and responsive learning communities and rigorous curriculum structures to enable teachers and students to make adventurous forays into the globally connected world in which we live.

Note

1 ANZAC Day commemorates the actions of Australian and New Zealand Army Corps soldiers in World War I.

4 Learning in integrated curriculum settings

Lenses, arguments and contexts

Inevitably, any discussion of integrated curriculum approaches turns to questions about learning – for example, what is being integrated, what is the relationship between integrated teaching and student learning, what kinds of learning, how can learning be measured, and, importantly, are integrated approaches more effective than disciplinary teaching? Although the literature is replete with plausible testimonials, the evidence remains inconsistent regarding the learning benefits of an integrated approach to curriculum. In a review of the literature from the 1940s to the early 1990s, Vars (1991) found more than 80 normative or comparative studies reporting that, on standardized achievement tests, students in various forms of integrated programmes performed better than, or at least as well as, students enrolled in separate subjects. Conversely, Marsh (1993) tracked some of the major research on integration from the US, the UK and Asia over the previous 50 years and found that there was limited evidence of either a positive or a negative effect.

More recently, Hurley (2001) presented evidence from a meta-analysis of 31 studies of student achievement in integrated classrooms compared with achievement in the core science curriculum. Quantitative analysis showed that students in the integrated classes outperformed those in traditional science classes, with small to medium effect sizes. Hurley found an average effect size for science achievement over 21 studies was 0.37 (standard error = 0.12). Importantly, she found that different forms of curriculum integration could have either a positive or a negative effect with regard to science achievement. The most positive effects were evident in the more deep-seated forms of integration, described by Hurley (2001) as 'total' or 'enhanced'.

While Applebee *et al.* (2007) found a strong correlation between more highly integrated content and cognitively engaging instruction, they concluded that 'interdisciplinary study is neither a problem nor a panacea' (p. 1036) in efforts to increase student achievement. Similarly, in a review of the literature, Czerniak (2007) concluded that 'the call for research that provides evidence of student performance through the use of integration has been met *somewhat* in the last few years' (p. 545, emphasis added). It appears the research is ambivalent about the outcomes of integrated approaches to curriculum, inviting a more detailed and nuanced examination of the effects of interdisciplinary approaches. Such an examination of learning effects is compounded by two underlying problems, namely the definition problem and the measurement problem.

The definition problem

Part of the problem in measuring the effectiveness of integrated approaches, we suggest, lies in the problem of defining what is meant by the term 'integration'. In our own work, we found a broad spectrum of classroom practices in Australian and Canadian schools that were described by teachers as being integrated (we gave an overview of these classroom practices in Chapter 2). We noted that these practices ranged across what Drake (1998) referred to as a continuum through multidisciplinary, interdisciplinary and transdisciplinary orientations, each involving fewer distinctions between subjects. Similar schema, based on the notion of continua, include from fragmented to shared (Fogarty, 1991) and correlated, shared and reconstructed (Applebee *et al.*, 2007). What these categorizations have in common is a graduated shift in thinking from the position that school subjects are natural entities to the position that they are social constructs. In the former orientation the subject is the starting point for curriculum organization, and in the latter the curriculum is organized around 'real world' problems, issues or projects, more or less independent of subjects.

These practical distinctions are also reflected in philosophical thinking about curricula. Young and Gehrke (1993), for example, claimed that 'we do not need to create the [curricular] whole: the whole already exists, we are in it. What we need to develop is our "initness", and the disciplines do not prepare us for that at all' (p. 447). Hatch (1998) pointed out that the division of knowledge into subjects for teaching and learning in schools is a legitimate part of our history and a pragmatic method of curriculum delivery. By contrast, Beane (1995) proposed that the curriculum should begin with the 'problems, issues and concerns posed by life itself', and that the central focus 'is the search for self- and social meaning' (p. 616). In a similar way, Rogers (1997) argued for a curriculum that uses a sense of knowledge based in the real world and in the child's experience. Clark (1997) envisaged a learner-centred curriculum which prioritized 'the connectedness of things' that could 'bridge the chasm ... between the classroom and the world beyond its doors' (p. 39).

In summary, while curriculum integration is often referred to as a single unified field, we suggest that it exists rather more like a large umbrella sheltering a multitude of related practices. The strength of the field lies in its capacity to embrace a broad range of practical and philosophical orientations, but it is also a major weakness when it comes to describing the learning outcomes of integration. The definition problem means that integration does not easily fit within a single and agreed set of descriptors; nor does integration lead to a single and agreed set of learning outcomes.

The measurement problem

The second problem is related to measurement. The measurement problem is reflected in the relatively narrow range of assessment practices and orientations used to measure and describe student learning in integrated settings, typically driven by measures of content matter. Such measures are not always well aligned with integrated teaching practices and inevitably lead to particular kinds of conclusions about learning. Hurley (2001), for example, limited her meta-analysis to quasi-experimental research that measured achievement in the disciplines of science and/or mathematics. Perkins and Simmons (1988) noted that assessment of learning in integrated settings characteristically neglects all but the content, and urged more attention to assessment of problem-solving and inquiry skills. Some studies have attempted to incorporate broader and more holistic perspectives into their evaluation of student learning, focusing on outcomes such as student motivation, attitude, cooperation, and capacity to transfer and apply knowledge. Ross and Hogaboam-Gray (1998), for example, found that Year 9 Canadian students studying an integrated science, mathematics and technology course improved their ability to apply shared learning outcomes, motivation, ability to work together and attitudes to appraisal of group work. Similarly, Hargreaves *et al.* (2001) found that middle-school students involved in an integrated curriculum demonstrated skills such as higher-order thinking, problem solving, application to real world problems, creativity and invention, and collaborative and individual learning. Davis (2004) argued that understanding students' learning is 'more than the measurement of their acquisition of facts and skills. Understanding student learning involves having a sense of students' development of identity' (p. 5).

An important step in resolving the measurement problem is to broaden our perspective on learning in integrated settings. For example, it is important to understand and accept that integrated approaches will incorporate a legitimate mix of *both* disciplinary *and* interdisciplinary objectives. Integrated issues and problems require the application of the cognitive and practical tools of the disciplines, including subject matter knowledge and rigorous explanations, as well as a range of cross-disciplinary knowledge and skills, such as problem solving, creativity and argumentation. Measurement tools need to reflect this diversity in an authentic way – requiring robust measures of disciplinary understanding and new kinds of measures of integrated knowledge.

*   *   *   *

It is this broadening of perspective that sets the tone for this chapter on learning in integrated curriculum settings. In doing so, we employ a Worldly Perspective on integration (introduced in the previous chapter) to examine teaching and learning in a variety of school contexts through multiple theoretical lenses. We believe that the theoretical lenses used to view the data should be consistent with the context of the classrooms in which the research is being conducted. We use the Worldly Perspective to discuss the findings of our work in a complex and multilayered way by taking into consideration the multiple forms of curriculum integration and the multiple ways student learning can be described. What follows is a chapter organized into three major sections, corresponding to three of our studies and three different ways of looking at learning. These sections are titled *learning lenses* (looking at learning through different theoretical lenses), *learning arguments* (looking at learning with respect to the major arguments or claims for integration), and *learning contexts* (looking at the relationship between classroom context and learning).

Learning lenses

A Worldly Perspective acknowledges and compensates for the possibility of different lenses and related arguments about learning in integrated curriculum settings. Three lenses on integrated learning that we have found useful in our work are an integrated lens, a disciplinary lens and a sources of knowledge lens. An *integrated* lens looks at interdisciplinary skills such as students' ability to transfer ideas from one context to another, the application of understandings to practical contexts, and students' general motivation and perception of the relevance of their school work. A *discipline-based* lens examines the extent to which students learn specific disciplinary concepts. A *sources-of-knowledge* lens focuses on how students access knowledge in order to make key learning decisions.

To explore these different lenses, we conducted a series of analyses of learning data from an Australian Year 9 integrated classroom at Eagleton Senior High School, where the students were working in pairs on a solar boat project. In this 10-week project, students were asked to design, build and test a boat that would be stable and propel itself by solar energy. In conducting the study, we were interested in the kinds of learning revealed by each lens – integrated, disciplinary and sources of knowledge – and the value of a multidimensional approach to understanding learning in integrated settings.

An integrated lens on learning

Using an integrated lens, our focus was on what the students learned that might be peculiar to integrated curriculum settings. This lens was underpinned by an epistemological analysis of curriculum by Rogers (1997). Rogers described certain ways of knowing as modes of thinking or conceptual tools used by experts, or student experts, when addressing complex problems. Rogers claimed that the dynamic experience of building and using knowledge when students are engaged in problem solving and active inquiry is often neglected and undervalued. A more practical manifestation of this lens is described in a detailed study, labelled a 'design experiment', by Roth (1998). Roth found that much of the children's learning in his case study of students in an engineering unit was not of the type traditionally valued in schools – 'the "knowing that" type' – of knowledge (p. 76). Rather, he found that children developed many competent practices that could be described as ' "know how to do" a variety of things' (p. 76). This 'knowing how to do' knowledge discussed by Roth is an example of the kind of learning that is the focus of our integrated lens on learning.

To conduct this analysis, we examined three learning episodes, each describing a pair of focus students working together on the solar boat project after being taught some of the basic science and mathematics principles behind boat design (for more details, see Venville *et al.*, 2000). One learning episode involved two students, Sharon and Cynthia, making decisions about the best solar cell circuit for their boat and how to attach it to their boat to maximize exposure to the sun. By testing and recording the results of various combinations of their cells in series and in parallel, Sharon and Cynthia found that connecting the cells in series would improve the voltage reading and connecting them in parallel would improve the current reading. They also learned that it is a combination of the current and voltage that influences the power and hence the final performance of their boat. The practical application of the students' understanding of Ohm's Law confounded the students because they didn't take into consideration the influence of a load on the circuit, so, in the end, they resorted to more pragmatic methods of finding out 'how to do' the circuit by asking other students. The knowledge gained from their mathematics class about how to read a sun chart and mathematical knowledge of trigonometry enabled Sharon and Cynthia to work out the optimum angle to mount the solar panels on their solar boat for the time of year and the time of day that the final testing took place.

Using an integrated lens, the curriculum enacted by the teachers of these students bridged the compartmentalized knowledge that is usually presented in discrete subject disciplines. Sharon and Cynthia's experience exemplified this bridging of knowledge as the students were able to use the language from science and from mathematics and apply their understandings from these disciplines to help them establish maximum power for their solar boat. We found that through this 'bridged knowledge' the integrated technology project provided a point of application, meaning, context and relevance for the concepts and skills the students studied in the three learning areas of science, mathematics and technology. The problem solving required for the solar boat project was the driving force behind most of what the students did in each of the subjects. The students were engaged in active inquiry because concepts were being used to address complex problems. By using an integrated lens in this study we found that students' learning was enhanced as a consequence of the bridged knowledge and the applied nature of the project.

A disciplinary lens on learning

For this second analysis (see Venville, Rennie and Wallace, 2003) we used a discipline-based lens, focusing on robust understandings of important phenomena and concepts within the discipline (in this case, of science). We were interested in students' conceptual understanding of science – particularly the concepts of 'circuit' and 'current' – and how they applied those understandings to their solar boat project. We prepared narrative-style anecdotes documenting the conceptions held by each individual student about circuit and current. The data were obtained through multiple-choice (forced response) style interview questions about the science concepts and open-ended interview questions that further probed the students' understanding and reasoning. Field notes of classroom observations and student portfolio data were used to build the narratives about the application of the concepts to the process of building the solar-powered boat.

We found that students had a clear, scientifically appropriate awareness that a closed circuit was required for current to flow. Without this understanding the students would not have been able to build a working solar boat. However, we were surprised to find that all six interviewed students had a consumption (non-scientific) view of electric current. For example, one student, Kevin, held a consumption view of electric current so strongly that he was sure that tests would indicate that the current would be reduced once it 'had been past the light bulb'.

Through the discipline-based lens, there was evidence to suggest that the students had a good understanding of some aspects of electricity, such as the concept of circuit. There also was clear evidence that their understanding of the concept of current was inconsistent with the accepted scientific view. The consumption view of electrical current held by the students was likely reinforced by the practical, applied nature of the technology project. It would seem that the students were able to solve problems with limited scientific conceptual tools. Rather like the electrical tradesperson who routinely solves practical electrical problems without sophisticated theoretical knowledge, these students constructed their boats with naïve understandings of electricity.

A sources-of-knowledge lens on learning

In the third analysis (see Venville, Rennie and Wallace, 2004), we used a sources-of-knowledge lens, focusing on the process of decision making and how students utilized various sources of knowledge. Our purpose here was to investigate how students sought and used knowledge to make key decisions about the solar boat project. We were also interested in how science and mathematics content knowledge was valued by the students as they carried out their projects.

The data in this third part of the study consisted of three embedded, narrative cases describing students' critical decisions about hull design, circuit design and solar cell mount design. Each case consisted of a lesson précis constructed from field notes of classroom observations, a vignette of the students' decision-making process constructed from field notes of classroom observation and transcripts of student interviews, and a diagrammatic representation of sources of information used by the pairs of students to make their decisions. The diagrammatic representations were initially constructed from the vignettes and cross-checked with the raw field notes and transcripts. The diagrammatic representations provided a crude indication of the chronology of the decision-making process and when the various sources of knowledge were used.

We found that the students used several sources of knowledge to make key project decisions about the solar-powered boat. These sources included the content knowledge taught in science and mathematics lessons, the classroom teachers, data from trials and tests performed by the students during lessons, students from the class and students and other people, such as family members, from outside the classroom. The extent to which the students relied on various sources of information also seemed to be directly linked with the degree of open-endedness of the problem that the students were attempting to address. We observed that the students tended to have a pragmatic approach to sourcing information, seeking out ways of obtaining potentially 'good', or workable, solutions to their problem.

Our findings from this third perspective confirmed those of Reiss and Tunnicliffe (1999) and Roth (1998), that people outside the classroom, such as family members, as well as teachers and classmates, are valued and regularly used sources of knowledge. Further, we found evidence of adaptive help-seeking strategies (Newman and Schwager, 1992) being used by the students in this project to self-regulate their learning. The integrated solar-powered boat project provided a context in which the students were academically challenged because they didn't know the answers and hence went to a range of sources of knowledge to find solutions. Moreover, the students showed sufficient curiosity and interest in their work that they were motivated to seek information from those sources of knowledge. According to Newman and Schwager (1992), this practice indicates that they were striving for independent mastery; that is, they wanted to learn in order to master a task, or solve the problem at hand, rather than for some extrinsic reason, for example, to satisfy the teacher or get good grades.

Lenses revisited

One 'why' question that leaps from this juxtaposition of the three theoretical lenses is, why is it that through an integrated lens, learning by the students was seen to be enhanced beyond what they would learn in the individual subjects, but using a disciplinary lens showed that none of the students understood the concept of current? Judging by the amount of research that has been conducted on the teaching and learning of the concept 'current', it is a concept highly valued by the science education community. It is commonly found in science curriculum documents around the world. From a science discipline perspective, the concept of 'current' is worth knowing and understanding.

Paradoxically, however, this concept was of little value in helping the students to construct and race their solar-powered boat. According to Czerniak, Weber, Sandmann and Ahern (1999), 'integration can be justified only if the understanding of content is enhanced and if integration is the best way to teach concepts' (p. 428). If we adopt the view of these authors the integrated approach to curriculum we found at Eagleton cannot be justified, because it did not enhance the understanding of important scientific concepts such as current. This seems to us to be a limited view in that learning, viewed through other lenses, such as an integrated lens and a sources-of-knowledge lens, took place even when conceptual learning was not optimal. These alternative lenses demonstrated that the students at Eagleton were involved in active inquiry and application of concepts in meaningful, relevant contexts. They were intrinsically motivated and pursued adaptive help-seeking strategies to learn from various sources of knowledge in order to master the task of building a solar-powered boat.

What this study shows is that learning outcomes vary depending on the lens used to view it. It is likely that a standard subject matter assessment framework would have revealed some disappointing results. However, when combined with some more integrated assessment frameworks, students were seen to apply knowledge in appropriate and effective ways and to draw from a variety of sources to complete the task at hand. This approach to learning and assessment is consistent with the Worldly Perspective whereby multiple theoretical lenses are used to examine learning in different integrated settings.

Learning arguments

Thinking about learning from a Worldly Perspective (that is, a framework that values a variety of learning lenses) invites alternative ways of judging the value of integrated programmes. Another approach, proposed by Ross and Hogaboam-Gray (1998), is to evaluate the integrated programmes against the major arguments for integration found in the literature on curriculum and learning. According to these authors, three arguments in particular relate directly to effects on student achievement. These are the *transfer* argument (that integration assists students' capacity to apply knowledge across different settings), the *focus* argument (that integration concentrates learning on a few big important ideas) and the *motivation* argument (that integration enhances enthusiasm for learning).

These three arguments suggest that integrated practices could increase student learning in a number of ways. But it is not always straightforward. For example, in our work at Eagleton we showed that a cross-disciplinary project approach led to some student misconceptions about the scientific concept of electrical current. As Ross and his colleague (1998) point out, integration may actually 'lead teachers to lose track of the structure of the disciplines, and their internal organization of ideas and principles' (p. 1121). Further, emphasizing horizontal connections (across subjects) may actually work against the year-by-year vertical scaffolding of disciplinary ideas, leading to curriculum fragmentation rather than integration.

In Stage Three of our series of studies, we used these three arguments for integration as a framework to examine the learning benefits of integration at two school sites in one of Canada's largest public school systems (see MacMath, Wallace and Chi, 2008a, 2008b). At the first site, Rinkview Public School, we observed a pod of two teachers and 50 Year 8 students who were engaged in a 6-week toy-building project. During this time, students experimented with simple machines, surveyed other students in the school about the kinds of toys they would like to buy, and then designed, built and marketed (to their peers) a moving toy. We watched the class as a whole, conducted close observations (recording on/off task behaviour and type of activity) of, and interviews (pre-, during and post-) with, 12 focus students in three homogeneous achievement groups, and also surveyed the whole class at the end of the project. At the second site, Greenwich Public School, one teacher and 26 Year 6 students worked on a thematic ice hockey unit. During the 5-week project, students designed an ice hockey season schedule, assembled travel information and brochures, and constructed an ice rink unit (including lighting and sound systems) to scale. For this site we focused our observations and interviews (pre-, during and post-) on 10 students in two mixed achievement groups, and administered a post-project survey to the whole class.

The transfer argument

The transfer argument refers to 'the ability of students to apply their knowledge when and where it is needed' (Ross and Hogaboam-Gray, 1998, p. 1120). The transfer argument is underscored by the idea that a range of cross-disciplinary instructional and learning experiences broadens (rather than narrows) the context in which knowledge is situated. It is argued that the kind of problem solving often found in integrated programmes promotes the transfer of knowledge from one subject to another. This transfer is more likely to occur in what have come to be called 'authentic' learning situations, dominated by open inquiry and project-centred activities where subject boundaries are blurred.

In terms of transfer, the two case study sites provided ample evidence of student creativity and adaptability in carrying out the various tasks. Whether designing, building and marketing the toy or building the hockey rink, most students were able to find alternative ways to overcome potential problems with materials, instruments, time, peers, etc. The open-endedness of the tasks seemed to provide sufficient scope for students to transfer general problem-solving skills (such as trial and error, negotiation, time management, accessing resources, material manipulation) from one task situation to another, and to eventually create a workable final product or model (within the broad parameters set by the teachers).

At Rinkview, for example, one group initially decided to build a toy car; however, after several lengthy discussions and negotiations about the type of materials required, concerns that other groups were also building cars, and unease about the complexity of the task (only one member, William, felt confident about building and using a motor), they decided to build a Buzz Fly, a device for propelling a styrofoam ball over a distance. The idea for this device came from another group member, Alex, who owned a toy based on a similar operating principle. Different members brought various raw materials from home, and the toy was constructed and trialled successfully prior to the final marketing day.

At Greenwich, the members of one group decided to divide up the task of building the hockey rink. One member, Arena, took the lead on scaling the rink to size and on the aesthetics of the rink, with Toby and Michael responsible for the electrical circuits to operate the lights and buzzer. After one attempt to build the rink to scale, it became apparent that the ratio of the length and width of their model was incorrect when compared with pictures of actual rinks found on websites, and so the group remade their rink from scratch. Initially, Toby and Michael, not realizing the importance of the need for a closed circuit, could not get their buzzer to work. However, after some trial and error, and advice from the teacher, they built two working series circuits, one for lights and another for the buzzer.

While most students were adept at general problem solving, there was less evidence of students' capacity to transfer specific knowledge to other situations. For example, at Rinkview, the teachers explicitly taught the characteristics of levers, expecting that students would apply this knowledge to the construction of their toy. While several of the students could recall (when asked) the technical features of levers, few applied this knowledge during the building of their toy. Further, during the final interview, only three of the 12 focus students could transfer this knowledge to explain the workings of another toy (a mouse trap car). In a further example, at Greenwich, while students had sound understandings of the mathematical principles of scale and most could solve routine problems involving scale, they were challenged when it came to building a scale model of a hockey rink on a styrofoam sheet. Several class groups converted the length by using a short-cut method of converting metres to centimetres; however, most students did not understand that they were using a ratio of 1:100. When they cut the sheet to length, they used the width of the sheet as it was without realizing that the ratio of length to width would be incorrect. Students encountered additional difficulties when adding extras to their rink (scoreboards, lights, nets, etc.). Rather than building the items to scale, students simply used the building materials as provided.

The focus argument

The focus argument, wrote Ross and Hogaboam-Gray (1998), 'is based on the belief that students are more likely to learn when their attention is focused on a few objectives or big ideas rather than diffused among many' (p. 1120). They referred to three aspects of this argument. First, that integration can potentially focus on a few big, shared ideas or topics, rather than a myriad of smaller and often unrelated discipline-based concepts. Second, because some subjects are supposedly complementary, tools from one subject can be used to enhance learning in another subject area. For example, science and mathematics may contribute to technology learning by providing students with some conceptual and process skills to solve technological problems (and vice versa). A final aspect of the focus argument concerns the potential for integration to highlight the quintessentials of each subject. It is suggested that, paradoxically, teaching in an integrated manner may actually assist students to comprehend and understand the traditions of individual subjects, including knowledge organization, key concepts, what counts as evidence and truth warrants. While the claimed advantages of this facet of integration are subject to debate (Lederman and Niess, 1998), some claim that integration may help students to understand how different subjects use different disciplinary approaches to solve problems (Tirosh and Stavy, 1992).

In examining our two cases, we found that the issue of focus is more complex than that imagined within the literature. Rather than emphasizing clarity, purpose, complementarity and quintessentials, the two projects were characterized by a multitude of different goals and expectations. The teachers, for example, hoped that the projects would serve some of the purposes set down by the provincial curricula (in terms of science, mathematics, social studies, etc.) and help the students achieve some (usually vaguely articulated) cross-curricular goals (such as applying knowledge to 'real life') as well as complete or build the final unit (the toy or the hockey rink). At different times during the projects, the teachers emphasized different aspects of the unit. For example, at Rinkview, after the students had conducted a peer survey on the marketability of their toy, the teachers taught a lesson on the mathematical principle of central tendency to help students organize their survey data. The teachers also taught formal lessons on the characteristics of levers in the hope that this knowledge would be applied in the construction of the toy. In building the toy, the students were asked to focus on several aspects, including design, aesthetics, workability and marketability. Again, in the second case, there were multiple foci. Embedded in the several thematic components – such as choosing a team name and logo, selecting players, creating a season schedule and building a model ice rink – were a number of knowledge expectations, such as ratios, decimals and fractions, means, and electric circuits. The teacher also repeatedly expressed her desire to develop in students a passion for (ice) hockey.

For the students, this diffuseness of goals led to some confusion over focus. While students exhibited high levels of on-task behaviour, at times the tasks seemed more fragmented than integrated. Sometimes, students were unsure whether to focus their energies on the final product or to spend time on the specific (and sometimes only vaguely connected to the final product) tasks set by the teachers along the way. Teachers also seemed conflicted about the goals of the unit, citing provincial curriculum expectations, broad goals such as critical thinking, as well as practical task expectations. At Rinkview, for example, the teachers expected the students to complete various tasks, including classifying levers, drawing graphs to report the results of the market survey and detailing the trials of the performance of the toy. These various tasks were also reflected in the time allocated by the 12 focus students – 25 per cent on designing and making the toy, 15 per cent on calculating the central tendency of their marketing survey results, 18 per cent on preparing charts of those results, 10 per cent on learning scientific terminology, and so on. When it came to the final product, it was somewhat unclear whether the principal focus was on the design and build aspect or the marketing aspect of the toy. Moreover, some students were unsure about the features of the final product; at Greenwich, for example, there was some uncertainty about whether the focus should be on the aesthetics or the scale dimensions of the hockey rink.

The motivation argument

The motivation argument is based on the idea that students are switched on to learning through working on meaningful tasks that are connected to their social and personal concerns (Hargreaves and Moore, 2000). Curriculum integration is said to encourage 'students to access less favoured subjects through more favoured ones' (Ross and Hogaboam-Gray, 1998, p. 1121). For example, locating and focusing the curriculum around so-called 'real world' situations may provide a point of entry to students who are otherwise switched off by traditional and more abstract subjects. Further, it is argued that integration may also expand opportunities for students to work together in situations of high motivation and participation (Cumming, 1996). For example, project- and problem-based approaches typically promote group activities, which have the potential to increase student engagement.

In this study, we looked at a number of indicators of motivation, including on-task behaviour and survey responses. In terms of student on-task behaviour for the toy-making unit, over 26 hours of observation, we found that the 12 focus students averaged 83 per cent (range 70–96 per cent) of class time engaged in on-task behaviour. These students were most on-task when conducting the survey of their peers. For the hockey unit, over 33 hours of observation, the 10 focus students were on-task for an average of 84 per cent (range 69–94 per cent) of class time, with the highest levels of engagement when determining the salaries and schedule of their hockey team. At Rinkview and Greenwich, the students were working in groups for 79 per cent and 51 per cent of class time, respectively. These levels of on-task behaviour and group work are remarkably high when compared with some of the classic studies of student engagement in regular classrooms (e.g., Sirotnik, 1983).

Table 4.1 Class means and standard deviations for levels of agreement on statements about an integrated unit

Statement	Rinkview[a]		Greenwich[b]	
	Mean[c]	SD	Mean	SD
The work we did in this unit was interesting	3.1	0.8	3.5	0.6
I enjoyed studying this unit	3.1	0.7	3.5	0.5
I would like to do more of this kind of work	3.1	0.9	3.5	0.6
The work we did in this unit was fun	3.2	0.7	3.5	0.8
It is important to me to be able to solve the kinds of problems we had in this unit	3.1	0.7	3.4	0.6

[a] Rinkview, $n = 50$.
[b] Greenwich, $n = 26$.
[c] Means are for a 4-point scale: 1 = strongly disagree, 2 = disagree, 3 = agree, 4 = strongly agree.

Another indicator of motivation levels is revealed in student responses on the class survey. Overall, students showed high levels of agreement (on a 4-point scale from 1, strongly disagree to 4, strongly agree) with statements about the motivational aspects of the unit. The class means and standard deviations for responses to the statements from students at Rinkview ($n = 50$) and Greenwich ($n = 26$) are reported in Table 4.1. All means exceed 3 and at Greenwich they are mostly 3.5, indicating strong agreement.

Post-unit interview data from the 22 focus students from the two classes provided confirmatory evidence for the overall high levels of student motivation. Typical comments were related to the fun aspect, working together in groups, the opportunity to build things, and having the subjects come together: 'It was really fun dividing up the work, and then doing everything and seeing how it comes together when the whole group does it'; 'All the activities are together in one, so we don't have different subjects at different times'; '[I liked] being a manager or something, building things, pretty fun'; '[It was like being] an electrical engineer [using] lights and anything to do with math'; and 'It was fun, because that's to get our hands [busy] … good to like, build things and test things'.

Arguments revisited

These two case studies of student learning in integrated classrooms reveal both the potential and the challenges of this kind of curriculum integration. In terms of student motivation, the students in these classrooms were well engaged, as indicated by very high levels of on-task behaviour. They expressed enjoyment, saw the relevance and importance of the work, appreciated the integrated aspects of the unit and generally liked working in groups to solve problems.

In terms of transfer, the relative open-endedness of the tasks appeared to allow students to use and cultivate general (problem-solving) skills to complete the final task. Transfer of other more (subject) specific knowledge was less evident. Students were not as confident in applying core ideas such as ratio, percentage, levers and circuits. Part of the problem here, we suspect, lies in diffuseness of focus. The teachers (and hence the students) were somewhat conflicted about the goals of the units, and uncertain at times about whether to focus on final products or other related (mainly disciplinary) knowledge and skills. Students and teachers were also pulled back and forth between knowing and doing, disciplinary and inter/transdisciplinary, mathematics and science, compulsory and optional (in terms of provincial expectations), fun and serious, etc. While these tensions may be resolved in part by a clearer task definition, we suspect that uncertainty about the focus is part of the continuing landscape of curriculum integration. We conclude by suggesting that there is some encouraging evidence of strong student learning in these particular integrated curriculum settings, with more work necessary to understand the complex relationship between learning transfer, focus and motivation.

Learning contexts

A further consideration in the debate about the relationship between curriculum integration and student learning is the impact of school, or more specifically, classroom context. In Pang and Good's (2000) study of integrated programmes, the authors suggested that 'many contextual factors may significantly affect the success or failure of the integrated approach' (p. 77). Broader contextual factors may include teacher recruitment and identity, subject histories, assessment structures, department politics, subject status, student futures, and an overcrowded and content-laden curriculum (Hargreaves *et al.*, 1996). In Chapter 3 we referred to several key contextual attributes impacting on the success or otherwise of an integrated programme, including small and stable learning environments, leadership, team activities linked to the classroom, in-school planning time, flexible timetable and community links.

School and classroom context could provide a further explanation as to why the results of empirical research about the impact of integrated approaches to curriculum on learning are so equivocal. In Stage Three of our research (see Venville *et al.*, 2008), we examined the effects of context in two Australian schools participating in a national programme to design and implement science-based projects to promote scientific literacy and awareness in students and their community. Each project was focused on a local community topic or issue and the science was used as a means of enriching students' science educa-tion through project-based learning.

Our two focus schools in this study – Brampton High School and Kentish Middle School – were in partnership with three other schools within the same region, a local university, a local government organization and the state water authority on an umbrella project about sustainable living. Each of the five schools developed an integrated project about sustainable living – in the cases of Brampton and Kentish, the projects were about midge (a small flying insect) and water nutrients, respectively. The focus of the project at Brampton was 'Midge in the Local Environment', and the science teacher used a variety of teaching strategies including formal lessons on food chains, food webs, energy transfer and biomass, a guest speaker, an excursion to the local lake, a research assignment in the library, some group work, individual worksheets and a final topic test. At Kentish, the topic 'Nutrification in the Wonthella Lake' was jointly taught by the science coordinator and the society and environment (social studies) coordinator. Lessons consisted of a combination of role-play, games, field excursions to the lake, laboratory work (including nutrient testing), poster analysis, modelling and project work.

Learning in context

What we observed in the classroom at Brampton High School was a teaching and learning culture organized around adherence to the principles, practices and academic rigour (or rules) of the subject. The school was organized into subject departments, the classroom timetable revolved around the subjects, the teacher was trained as a secondary science teacher and the major class assessment was the common Year 9, end-of-topic science test. The student learning in the classroom at Brampton tended to be about the concepts and skills that are traditionally addressed within the discipline of science. Prior to the project, student narratives about midge were personal, relating to how the midge get into the nose, hair and mouth, and where swarms of midge can be seen. After the project, students still talked about these personal experiences but they also talked about scientific concepts from the life and living expectations of the state curriculum framework, such as insect life cycles, food chains and food webs. They related what they had learned about the science principles of ecology to the midge by discussing the food chain from algae to midge, frogs and tiger snakes.

The context and curriculum at Brampton were focused on helping students to understand the science expectations set out in the state curriculum document and apply them to a 'real world' issue. Students did not consider the broader social, aesthetic and political aspects of the midge problem and the values inherent in the methods that are used to control the midge. In this sense students' learning might be considered limited to scientific concepts, rather than a more holistic understanding of midge ecology.

At Kentish Middle School, the educational context in the classroom reflected a strong focus on the core, shared values regarding the education of the adolescent child. The school was structured into learning communities led by teams of teachers, the physical structure of the classroom was open, the timetable was blocked but flexible, with time for collaborative teacher planning, and the assessment was individualized, integrated and applied.

At Kentish, the student learning encompassed the broad, global idea of the impact of human activity on the lake environment. Concepts were explored and reinforced in science, society and environment, and other learning areas. Prior to the project, the student narratives about the lake reflected their personal experiences of visiting the lake, having picnics, and engaging in activities such as walking the dog. After the project, the narratives indicated that students were more aware of plant and animal diversity than previously, could discuss factors impacting on the health of the lake, such as pollution, phosphate, garbage and salinity, were aware of public responsibility for the lake and could make suggestions about how to improve their environment. There also was evidence that they could apply these ideas to different contexts.

The students in the classroom at Kentish demonstrated learning that was focused through the external-to-the-classroom, local issue of the health of the lake, and drew on the disciplines as sources of knowledge to develop understanding about the lake problem. The survey and questionnaire results indicated students' learning was not rigidly focused on the concepts taught in science, for example, on aquifers and salt concentrations, but on the more global attitudes and values embedded in those concepts, such as human action that can limit salinity problems. The distinction between subjects was not clearly defined, nor was this perceived to be relevant, as the survey and interviews indicated that students often referred to ideas and activities taught in society and environment, science, English and other learning areas when discussing the lake.

It could be argued that learning, such as strengthened values and attitudes towards the environment, is amorphous, not belonging to or developing conceptual knowledge within any particular discipline to an appropriate level. This kind of learning also could be considered to have no clear form or structure, as students within the same class demonstrated inconsistency in the concepts with which they were familiar. Some students knew about salinity and/or phosphate, whereas others did not. Such inconsistency within integrated units of work was also observed by Ritchie and Hampson (1996). This kind of learning, therefore, is often considered difficult to define and, more importantly, difficult to measure or test in an objective way.

Context revisited

Like the general literature on curriculum integration, our findings from this study demonstrate ambivalence. When viewed from an integrated perspective, the project in the classroom at Kentish could be considered to be successful because the degree of integration between subjects was greater than that observed at Brampton. But if we examine the findings using a science discipline-based lens, the project at Brampton could be considered to be highly successful. The students' learning was focused on a defined area of content, and assessed via the science topic test on ecology. The learning outcomes at Kentish, on the other hand, were less focused on science, more global in nature, and more difficult to test and measure.

When classroom contexts are considered, the different curriculum practices and learning outcomes observed in these two settings are not surprising. In adopting a Worldly Perspective, we do not conclude that one approach was better than the other, merely that they were different and that the differences can largely be attributed to the educational context. The nature of the integration, and consequently the nature of the student learning, was seen to fit the context. We agree with Hargreaves and colleagues (1996), who pinpoint the needs of the people, the purpose of the curriculum and how well it fits the setting as being important guidelines for designing an integrated curriculum.

On the basis of the findings of this comparative study, we speculate about the relationship between classroom context, curriculum integration and student learning. We believe that the educational context shapes (i.e., both enables and constrains) the nature of the curriculum integration that is enacted in a classroom. In turn, the approach to curriculum shapes the nature of the student learning that results. From a research perspective it is important to note the impact that contextual factors have on the conclusions that researchers might reach. If the classroom under scrutiny has a context that enables a highly integrated curriculum, and researchers view the learning using a disciplinary lens, it is likely that the outcomes will be disappointing. Similarly, if a classroom has a context that constrains the degree of curriculum integration, the implementation of integrated project may be judged to be inadequate. It is important therefore to take the broader view, to illuminate both the successes and the limitations of different approaches, and to acknowledge the importance of context.

Conclusions

We conclude this chapter with several observations about our studies of student learning in integrated curriculum settings. First, it is clear that integration suffers from what might be called a definition problem, thus confounding attempts to describe student learning in definitive terms. Integration incorporates a wide range of philosophical orientations, degrees of integration and classroom practices, with sympathetic links to many other related curriculum movements, such as problem-based learning, arts-based education, holistic education, global citizenship, environmental education, new basics, science and society, among others. We accept that this kind of healthy diversity will always be part of the integration landscape. However, integration diversity complicates attempts to make direct comparisons of learning in 'integrated' versus 'normal' classroom settings. At best, we can describe student learning in particular cases, being clear about the characteristics of that integrated practice, and being cautious about generalizing findings to all forms of integration.

Second, we highlight what we call the measurement problem. Essentially, this problem stems from a poor alignment between standard assessment tools and practices and the inter-disciplinary goals of integration. We found that teachers did not have the appropriate tools (and skills) to assess the kind of integrated practices that they were encouraging in their students, such as collaborative problem solving, creativity, networking, knowledge transfer, technological skills and real-world applications. Teachers typically employed standard subject-based rather than inter-disciplinary measures – often constrained by state and provincial guidelines for reporting on outcomes. The same problem, we believe, is to be found in research on learning in integrated classrooms, where many studies (including some of those summarized in the introduction to this chapter) rely on disciplinary measures to draw conclusions about the efficacy of integrated teaching and make comparisons with other approaches. As we found in our work at Eagleton, the conclusions drawn about student learning depend on the perspective taken and the tools used to measure learning. The theoretical lens is important as it signals what is valued and what is not. The challenge here is to find ways of making assessment and research more authentic, to more carefully align teaching and assessment lenses and practices, and to develop appropriate tools to measure and report on integrated learning.

Our third observation concerns the focus issue. Focus is one of the oft-quoted arguments for integration, the idea that students' attention will be focused on a few key ideas or goals rather than be diffused among many. The reality is that integrated units involve a merging and thus a conflation of goals. The big idea does not stand alone, but is served by a complex mix of technical, practical and critical knowing. And for teachers, the precious time set aside for an integrated topic must also be used to serve other (often tangentially related) curriculum priorities. The focus issue is evident in all cases described in this chapter, where students were expected to focus on the big idea or final product (solar-powered boat, hockey rink, toy, wetland management), certain disciplinary concepts (Ohm's Law, ratio, levers, midge life cycle, food chains, etc.), as well as a range of process skills (group work, problem solving, use of materials, developing community links). Our view is that some degree of focus diffuseness is part of the unpredictable nature of integrated classrooms. The challenge is to avoid focus confusion, to be clear about the parameters and expectations of the task/s at hand while allowing plenty of space for student creativity. At times, however, focus will also mean being explicit about some of the subsidiary goals of the project (such as certain subject matter understandings) and aligning the assessment practices accordingly.

Our fourth observation is that context matters. Context mattered in all of the schools that we studied. At Eagleton, Rinkview and Greenwich, combinations of factors (timetable flexibility, teacher interest, etc.) enabled teachers to work together or alone to plan and implement integrated units in various ways. At Brampton and Kentish we saw how a similar starting point, a brief to conduct a community-based science project, resulted in different processes and outcomes. Clearly school organization, timetable structure, curriculum and assessment orientations and teacher strengths are among the myriad contextual factors that influence the way in which integrated programmes are conducted, and the kind of outcomes to be expected. While in Chapter 3 we described how some key programme characteristics operate to support curriculum integration, here we acknowledge that integrated practices are conducted in a variety of contexts. Pragmatically, a Worldly Perspective recognizes that teaching practices will differ depending on the context, and allows that different learning outcomes may result. We suggest that integrated programmes should be judged on their merits, taking context into account and acknowledging the variety of possible interdisciplinary and disciplinary outcomes.

We now return to the central question of what is being learned in integrated curriculum settings. The answer is, it depends. It depends on how integration is defined, on the kind of integration being taught, and the lenses (and tools) used to view and assess learning. Such a response precludes generalized findings about the efficacy of integrated approaches and invites a more fine-grained analysis based on particular cases and particular frameworks. Looking at the cases in this chapter in terms of the frameworks of motivation, transfer and focus, for example, we have some reason for cautious optimism (and some reservations). In all cases, the students showed generally high levels of engagement, interest and curiosity. We found evidence of students' capacity to transfer general problem-solving skills. There were also some good examples of students bridging subject knowledge to the task at hand, although many struggled to make the connections with subject knowledge. Student learning success in our cases is also related to the issue of focus. Learning was enhanced when goals were made explicit and when assessment aligned with those goals.

Conclusions about the efficacy of integrated approaches must inevitably be equivocal. Those hoping that integration will also incorporate all the subject matter expectations that might otherwise have been covered will be disappointed. Those looking for an ideal integration world where the subjects are set aside will similarly be let down. The best we can hope for is a kind of hybridity where the result is less than one doubled (Bhabha, 1995). Student learning in these hybrid settings will incorporate a mix of knowledges – including knowledge of what, how, where and why; integrated and disciplinary; local and global; as well as technical, practical and critical. At times, some knowledges will be privileged over others, and at other times not. A Worldly Perspective is also a pragmatic one, accepting that integrated teaching and learning take place in multiple worlds. The curriculum challenge, as always, is to identify and clarify what knowledge is important to learn, scaffold students through the learning process and assess students authentically.

5 The status of school knowledge

Challenging the discipline-based structure

This chapter is about the nature of school knowledge, how it is organized in curricula and the status attributed to knowledge that is structured in different ways. Deciding on which knowledge counts and which doesn't is a socio-political process, steeped in the history and tradition of schooling and curriculum. In almost all educational jurisdictions, the dominant view of knowledge is that it is made up of disciplines such as science, language, history and mathematics, and that this structure is the most suitable way to organize the school curriculum. People who think outside this status quo, however, have presented strong arguments that knowledge in the real world is not compartmentalized into disciplines. They further argue that using this disciplinary approach to curriculum alienates students from understanding the way the real world works and prevents them from being able to apply their understandings to complex, authentic problems and issues of interest to them and the broader community. This chapter builds on the discussion of learning in the previous chapter and delves more deeply into the outcomes of disciplinary and integrated curricula. We explore the reasons why a disciplinary structure dominates school curricula, examine two case studies about alternative, integrated ways that school knowledge can be structured, and pose questions about the potential of integrated curricula to deliver knowledge that counts in a global community.

The structure of school knowledge

Wherever and whenever we attended high school, most likely we were immersed in an environment where we learnt the content and processes of school subjects such as history, mathematics and biology. As a consequence, it is difficult to imagine other ways that school knowledge can be presented. In this section of the chapter, we examine the relationship between the nature of school subjects and academic disciplines, the knowledge arguments for and against an integrated curriculum and the hegemony of the discipline-based structure of school knowledge.

Subjects and disciplines

It is the nature of the school subject that seems to us to hold the key to understanding the nature and structure of school curricula, so here we explore what is meant by a 'subject' and how it relates to the academic discipline it represents.

P. L. Gardner (1975) explained that it was possible, during the 1970s, to identify a common ideology that had guided the construction of curriculum documents. The ideology was related to a theory about the nature of academic disciplines and a desirable relationship between disciplines and their corresponding school subjects. This 'structure of knowledge theory' has been described in the writings of Bruner (e.g., 1960) and Schwab (e.g., 1964). According to P. L. Gardner, Bruner, Schwab and others, school subjects should serve as 'faithful and valid introductions to the academic disciplines whose names they bear' (Gardner, 1975, pp. 1–2). Gardner defined disciplines in the following way:

> Knowledge is produced by a variety of *disciplines* ... disciplines possess social reality: they consist of identifiable groups of people who work together, meet each other at conferences, travel to each others' laboratories, correspond with each other, write journal articles for each other, and decide who, and which ideas, they are prepared to admit to the club.
>
> (Gardner, 1975, p. 2, original emphasis)

Gardner (1975) argued that different kinds of knowledge statements are generated and validated by the discipline and that these demonstrate that different modes of thinking and reasoning are used in the disciplines. Rogers (1997) concurred: True disciplines are ways of knowing the conceptual tools, methods and validation criteria that experts use when addressing complex problems.

Rather than school subjects being introductions to academic disciplines, as proposed by the structure of knowledge theory, Stengel (1997) suggested that academic disciplines and school subjects have a range of possible relationships, including continuous, discontinuous and different-but-related. She argued that the manner in which stakeholders interpret the relationship between these concepts has a direct impact on curriculum in terms of purpose, practice and substance. More recently, Hameyer (2007) argued that domain knowledge in fields such as arts, linguistics, history or natural sciences is subject to the professional identities of their disciplinary participants and thus cannot be mirrored directly into the school curriculum. This perspective is not consistent with the structure of knowledge theory because, Hameyer explained, a school curriculum is the result of a complex transformation process and not just a matter of reducing quantities of content. According to Hameyer, this transformation process can take on several forms including the reconstruction, reconceptualization, selection, simplification and integration of content.

Rogers (1997) claimed that the translation of knowledge from the richness of disciplines to the superficial level of school subjects is problematic for several reasons, including the lack of attention to the active nature of learning, that there is no democratic or systematic method for determining what information is of most worth, and that it assumes that children learn by adding pieces of information to their knowledge systems, an assumption that is inconsistent with modern notions of learning and development. Rogers contrasted the richness of the disciplines with school subjects, where she claimed knowledge is presented as 'finished products' (p. 686) with no vitality, interdependence or intellectual content. In other words, the process of translating disciplinary knowledge into school subjects removes the inquiry and knowledge-building processes because the subjects are defined by content, including concepts, facts and topics that are disconnected from the modes of inquiry of the parent discipline (Rogers, 1997).

Regardless of these discussions about the relationship between discipline and school subject, we cannot ignore the importance of a discipline in defining the content and nature of a related school subject. In our modern, global society, however, the notion of an academic discipline is far from coherent. If we consider the discipline of science, for example, metaphors in the literature reflect both 'holistic', global science and the 'fragmented' nature of science. For example, Capra (1996) argued that the mechanistic, easily quantifiable models of science of a bygone era are in opposition to the holistic awareness of today's scientific phenomenon. Capra used biology as an example where, he explained, the cell can no longer be considered simply as a fundamental building block of life; rather it must be thought of in symbiotic partnership with organelles and other cells. Chaos theory, as described by Briggs and Peat (1999), encourages scientists to go beyond their mathematical and scientific origins and embrace myth, mysticism, poetry, literature, art, religion and philosophy and create an interconnected view of the universe, our world, our society and ourselves.

In stark contrast with the holistic views of science, others point to the fragmentation of 'science' into an array of sub-disciplines or specialities. Carter (2008) explored the implications of globalization for science education and noted the 'increase in the sheer size and scope of contemporary science research in increasingly fragmented sub-disciplines' (p. 625). Jenkins (2007) argued that while science in schools is promoted as a 'coherent curriculum component', in reality it 'fosters an untenable but enduring notion of a unifying scientific method that ignores important philosophical, conceptual, and methodological differences between the basic scientific disciplines' (p. 265).

Young (2008) claimed there is clear evidence for a growing and global emphasis in curricula on relevance, student choice, and responding to the needs of the individual learner. He questioned whether this tendency to more choice for students is as inclusive as was once assumed because many students may lack the cultural resources to make appropriate choices. Recent Australian research found that the declining proportion of enrolments in senior-level science subjects is due to a broad phenomenon which has seen similar falls in many traditional subject areas including economics, geography, history and advanced mathematics (Lyons and Quinn, 2010). These declines, according to Lyons and Quinn, are principally due to the responses of students 'to the greater array of options available in Year 11, resulting in proportionally lower enrolments in many long-standing subjects' (p. i). Moreover, Young (2008) noted a growing tendency across countries for reduction in the amount of technical or subject-specific content of curriculum programmes. The priorities of schooling appear to be changing from a focus on the acquisition of specialized, technical knowledge to a focus on the role of schools in the broad socialization of young people as future citizens.

Knowledge arguments for and against integrated curricula

The arguments supporting a disciplinary approach to curriculum tend to flow from the notion that disciplines provide specialized knowledge that enables rigorous explanation of clearly identified aspects of the world. In this way, disciplines create a sense of order about the complex world and provide students with the understandings and skills they need to solve focused, discipline-based problems (H. Gardner, 2004; Leonardo, 2004). For example, Gardner (2004, p. 233) argued:

> The disciplines are important human achievements. They are the best answers that human beings have been able to give to fundamental questions about who we are, physically, biologically, and socially.

Schoenfeld (2004) pointed to research that shows that 'disciplines matter in teaching and learning to teach' (p. 237), and that 'classroom activities must foster active engagement with the content and processes of the discipline, with students developing and testing ideas in ways consistent with the paradigms of the disciplines they study' (p. 238). Young (2008) claimed that 'knowledge that takes people beyond their experience has historically been expressed largely in disciplinary or subject forms' (p. 10), and suggested the disciplines are the epistemological price we pay for a better understanding of the world.

Elizabeth Blackburn, the 2009 Nobel Prize winner for discoveries in molecular biology, explained that deep specialist knowledge is needed for successful cross-disciplinary research such as that she carried out on cancer and chronic stress (Trounson, 2010). In an interview for *The Australian* newspaper's Higher Education Supplement, Blackburn argued against early generalization: 'My feeling is not to get too cross-disciplinary and shallow and spread all over the place too quick' (Trounson, 2010, p. 23). She believed that the key to success was that each of the scientists she collaborated with had deep knowledge of their respective fields and this created confidence and mutual respect. 'We had to explain stuff to each other, and sometimes I would think it incredibly elementary what they didn't know and I'm sure they thought it was incredibly elementary what I didn't know' (p. 23). Blackburn's research about telomeres, the protective caps on chromosomes, has provided better understanding of the relationship between chronic stress, ageing and cancer. With reference to her involvement in the cross-disciplinary work, she said that 'One needs to be able to bring something very substantive to the table because I can see the temptation would be to try to be overly generalized and shallowness would be the consequence' (Trounson, 2010, p. 23).

The alternative argument is that integrated approaches to curriculum enable students to better understand the realities of their experiences outside school (Leonardo, 2004). Integrated approaches to curriculum allow teachers and students to go beyond the ideas and problems that are usually presented within disciplines and respond to issues that may be more immediately relevant and motivating to young people (Beane, 1991).

Hargreaves and Earl (1990) argued that secondary schools are deeply entrenched in disciplinary structures simply for historical reasons and this creates an unbalanced curriculum that is content-driven and of limited relevance for many students. Supporters of curriculum integration argue that knowledge in the real world is holistic and the division of knowledge into subjects for teaching and learning in schools is simply a practical method of curriculum delivery that is carried through year after year (Hatch, 1998). Young and Gehrke (1993) pointed out the paradox of the phrase 'curriculum integration'. Curriculum integration is supposed to reflect the notion of wholeness and coherence, the totality and unity of existence. The paradox comes from the suggested need, particularly in school systems, to patch together the disciplines to create a whole. The whole does not need to be created. It already exists, they stated. Others have argued that learning for adolescents is about life experiences in familiar contexts and relationships and interactions they have with trusted people, and that compartmentalized, disciplinary knowledge and narrow reasoning processes are not consistent with this way of understanding knowledge (O'Loughlin, 1994).

The hegemony of the discipline-based structure of school knowledge

Goodson (1992) characterized the school subject in the British, American and Australian high-school curriculum as 'unchallengeable high ground' (p. 23) that hardly felt the effects of the waves of curriculum reform of the 1960s. Two decades later Goodson's words remain apt; throughout the western world, curriculum documents stand as evidence that the school subject is as strong as ever. The Australian Curriculum, Assessment and Reporting Authority (ACARA), for example, recently released the new national Australian Curriculum for learning areas including English, mathematics, science and history (ACARA, 2010). England introduced a National Curriculum in 1992 which defined a range of subjects to be taught as a core curriculum in all schools (Department for Employment and Education, 2000). Goodson (1992) pointed out the 'uncanny' resemblance of the core curriculum to the definition of public and grammar school subjects established in the 1904 Regulations and confirmed in the School Certificate Examinations of 1917. Siskin (1994) claimed that in English high schools the 'arrangement into (subject) departments has been ... taken for granted' (p. 9). During the last decade, more statutory subjects, including citizenship, were added, but in January 2011 a review of the National Curriculum was announced (Department for Employment and Education, 2011) to determine (among other things) the essential knowledge in English, mathematics and science. This is reminiscent of Kliebard's (1986) comments which characterized the school subject in the high-school curriculum as an 'impregnable fortress'.

The US Department of Education has National Education Standards arranged around seven subject areas, comprising fine arts, language arts, mathematics, physical education and health, science, social sciences and technology (National Research Council, 1996). The US National Science Education Standards identified eight science-content categories including: unifying concepts and processes, science as inquiry, science and technology, science in personal and social perspectives, and the history and nature of science. Bianchini and Kelly (2003) explained that while a standards-based curriculum was conceptualized by national reform efforts, 'it is the state rather than nation that exercises primary responsibility for organizing and overseeing public education' (p. 379). For example, core curriculum areas in the Californian standards reflect the discipline-based character of the national standards and include English-language arts, mathematics, history-social science and science (California Department of Education, 1999). In contrast with the national standards, however, the Californian standards document identified only four science-content standards: earth science, life science, physical science and investigation and experimentation. While the national standards identified eight science-content categories that do not align with the traditional sub-disciplines of science, at the state level in California the traditional school sub-disciplines of biological, physical, earth and investigative science predominated. According to Bianchini and Kelly (2003), the Californian standards are presented as 'long lists of scientific facts students are expected to know' (p. 380), and 'may not help students achieve greater scientific literacy, the goal of science education reform' (p. 383).

Roderick and Camburn (1999) commented on how the move from primary to secondary schools results in North American students having to cope with dramatic increases in the structure of academic schedules, including the movement from isolated subject to isolated subject. In a similar way, Rogers (1997) described entrenched subjects as a scheduling device rather than a programme of learning.

Regardless of the range of cultures and social structures in each of the countries described above, it would appear that subjects, based on traditional disciplines and sub-disciplines, provide a default structure to which curriculum developers regularly revert through cycles of reform. This is consistent with the structure of knowledge theory as described by P. L. Gardner (1975). We have found in our own research, however, strong and resilient teachers who have reconceptualized the way that school knowledge is structured and have persisted with excellent, highly integrated approaches to teaching and learning.

Alternative approaches to the structure of school knowledge

In this section of the chapter we describe two examples of teaching and learning where the curriculum structure was different from the traditional discipline-based approach. The first is a case study of a bridge project at Southern High School where students were required to design and construct a model bridge in much the same way as engineers would in the real world. The structure of the enacted curriculum in this case study was driven by the design brief provided by the teacher to the students, and discipline-based knowledge was utilized in an integrated way as it would be by the engineering profession. In a second case study we revisit the sustainability project at Kentish Middle School where students learned about and investigated the environmental health of a local wetland. The structure of the curriculum in this case study was driven by an important local issue, and knowledge from the discipline-based school subjects was drawn upon as needed by the students to enrich and develop their understanding of their local wetland.

Profession-based approaches: A case study of the bridge project

Rogers (1997) proposed the professions as an alternative approach to the structure of knowledge in school curricula. She argued that while the disciplines should play an important role in shaping the curriculum, they should not be seen as the only authority, and that 'other sources of authority' that can 'offer meaningful sources of knowledge and standards' (p. 700) should be taken into account when educators think about curriculum. Rogers explained that the professions, as well as the disciplines, have valuable sets of expectations and standards that students and teachers might use when trying to construct and validate understanding. As a profession with real-world relevance, Rogers promoted architecture as a 'source of authority' because it draws together knowledge from several disciplinary areas and operates according to its own set of standards. Rogers pointed out that architecture is particularly helpful in problem- and project-based curricula, where it can present an immediate set of standards by which student work can be evaluated:

> I want to pose possibilities for shaping the curriculum that stretch beyond what we recognize as either subjects or disciplines. Such alternatives, I believe, complement the explicit disciplinary knowledge of the academy

with a sense of knowledge that is rooted in the real world (in professions, for example, which do not have a direct counterpart in the academy) and in the child's experience. These alternatives, in sharing the authority of 'knowledge' among the real world, the academy and the child's experience, are more fully student-constructed and student-owned than the knowledge gained in either subjects or disciplinary knowledge. Such alternatives are meant to engage students in rigorous and deep learning, but also designed to encourage them to begin mapping their own understandings (discovering disciplinary and real-world frameworks of knowledge) as a result of their experiences, rather than as matters of fact set down by teachers.

(Rogers, 1997, p. 700)

In our own work, we observed a technology teacher at Southern High School, Ms O'Reilly, who involved her students in the design and construction of a model bridge using mathematical, scientific and design principles that seemed to reflect Rogers' (1997) call to recognize the professions as legitimate sources of knowledge around which to structure the curriculum. The technology studies course was a Year 9 (students aged 13 to 14 years) optional unit of two, one-hour lessons per week over five weeks. The course attracted a wide range of students, including some who were academically talented and others who were skilled with their hands. The class comprised 15 male students who worked in twos or threes to investigate, design and construct a model bridge, examining theory about forces and the forces involved in putting a load on a bridge. Ms O'Reilly said:

In the main I get good science students, I don't often get kids who are not interested. We don't necessarily get all bright kids but they are always interested and motivated. Some of them are very good at working with their hands and not good at the conceptual stuff, others are good at the conceptual stuff and not good with their hands and if we work out teams properly and you get a mixture of expertise, it can work out quite well.

The students were informed that an engineering company had gone bankrupt leaving one of their bridges unfinished, and they had to use the information they discovered about structures to complete the job. They were asked to produce a strong, aesthetically pleasing bridge, while minimizing the cost. Design criteria included a span of 750 mm with no support and a load capacity of two cartons of soft drink cans with a maximum of 25 mm vertical deflection under full load. The bridge was constructed from the materials on the official supply list with tools available in the workshop and cost under $150 in 'bridge bucks' (play money supplied by the teacher). The teacher explained the main expectation from the course in terms of students learning:

The main expectation for every module that I do is problem solving. So problem solving, there is critical thinking, there is analytical thinking, a big one is time management. Working as a team, being able to delegate the jobs that have to be done and managing that time. With the bridge project they do have a set period of time that they've got to finish it in. So we use that critical path to try and keep their time management under control.

The teacher also explained the conceptual expectations:

In terms of the conceptual stuff I really want them to realize that there is a structural shape that is stronger than another structural shape. So the theory of triangulation is important, they seem to manage to get that quite well. The other part associated with that is the theory of redundant members. So it's forces, it's opposite forces, or the theory of forces, it's beams and bending, it's the different types, structural types. Jointing systems associated with those.

Students completed several investigations into structures, beams and bending, joints and jointing, and were introduced to types of forces, the history of bridges and bridge types, before planning their bridges. The students designed, manufactured and evaluated their own bridge before the class evaluation, where prizes were awarded to the structure with the best strength-to-weight ratio, the most aesthetically pleasing bridge and the cheapest bridge that met all the design criteria. A prize also was awarded to the group who submitted the best written documentation of their project. As Ms O'Reilly explained,

There's also that aesthetic aspect that I try and bring in and I try and emphasize the importance of that by bringing in another teacher to do the judging of that and a teacher who can talk in aesthetic terms. So we're looking at the overall form, that's an important part that anyone can build, but can we build to make it look aesthetically pleasing as well as achieve the engineering criteria that have been set. There's always that design aspect that I try and bring in to it. It's a lot, if they can learn all those things in five weeks we're doing very well.

We observed and documented seven of the ten lessons, and interviewed five students one week after the completion of the course. Students were asked to describe their bridge, explain their design, say what they learnt during the project and give their opinion about the usefulness of their science and mathematics knowledge for the construction of the bridge. They were also questioned about their understanding of the forces acting when a load is placed on a bridge. The teacher was interviewed two weeks after the completion of the course about her general reflections on the bridge project. The data were analysed and case stories of the five students constructed (see Venville *et al.*, 1999b). An example of one of the case stories is included here.

Gavin

Gavin was described by Ms O'Reilly as creative and prepared to take a risk. She said that Gavin asked a lot of questions in class and would (lightheartedly) challenge her if he thought she had made a mistake. Gavin worked with another student, Colby, to make the bridge for this project and, like most of the other groups, they constructed a deck bridge from two pieces of plywood with 'I' beams in between. Gavin said they tested different beam structures with pop sticks at the beginning of the project and found that triangles and 'I' beams were strong but the triangles were too expensive so they decided to use 'I' beams.

Gavin and Colby spent considerable time during one lesson debating whether to spend more money strengthening their bridge or to make it more aesthetically pleasing. They also said they were wondering whether to do this at all, because the bridge was already strong and they could get a prize for spending less money. They decided to add suspension 'because it will add some strength and it doesn't cost very much'. Gavin had to work out the cost of the string. He wanted 3,000 mm of string and he knew that the string cost $1.00 for every 300 mm. He had difficulty doing the proportional problem to work out how much he had to pay. Ms O'Reilly helped him work out that the string would cost $10.00 by doing the cross multiplication on the blackboard. When he saw the calculation he said they do those all the time in mathematics.

Gavin and Colby decorated their bridge with dowel rods and string, spray painted it and covered the ends so that the internal 'I' beams were not visible. The students then covered the bottom of their bridge with corrugated cardboard 'to make it look good'. During testing, when two cartons of soft drink cans were placed on top of Gavin and Colby's bridge, it deflected slightly, but not more than the 25 mm limit. This group won the 'best looking bridge' competition, and the teacher from the English department who did the judging said that the suspension presented pleasing curves, that the bridge had slim, clean lines and the corrugated cardboard was interesting.

Gavin said that their biggest problem during construction was working out how to fix the top deck on their bridge. The glue from the hot glue gun dried too quickly, so they decided to use PVA glue even though this meant the bridge had to be clamped and left to set. They also had difficulty reinforcing some screws and they solved that problem by drilling them into the 'I' beams. The students only spent 100 of the 150 bridge bucks they were allocated and Gavin said they could have spent less but decided to spend some on decoration. Gavin felt that learning about the 'I' beams and triangles being strong structures was important and that his mathematics knowledge was useful for measuring. He also said that his scientific knowledge was useful for finding out a lot about using the 'I' beams and the triangles.

When asked during the interview about the forces acting in a diagram, Gavin said that they were 'static' forces because 'it's just holding up itself like by the strength of the wood or whatever the materials are'. When asked if the forces had any direction, Gavin said that 'mainly it's just, well, the load is pushing down, but it won't go down unless it was going to snap'. The interviewer asked Gavin why the load stays there and he answered, 'because of the strength of the bridge'. When asked if there is a force acting up on the load he said, 'I suppose, the strength of the bridge would be pushing up ... that would even out until there was a larger load here, then it would overcome this one, which is a set load I suppose, and it would push down and it would break'.

The results of this case study provided considerable information about students' learning in a technology-based, integrated environment. There was evidence to suggest that the practical, technological experience of the bridge-building project precipitated important scientific understandings about forces for the majority of the students. For example, all interviewed students recognized that there were forces in action in the diagrams used in the interview, even though there is no suggested movement in any of these diagrams. The results of this study contradict the findings from other research (e.g., Clement, 1987) that the majority of students of this age associate forces only with movement. In addition, three of the five interviewed students, including Gavin, recognized that forces were acting in opposite directions. Two students, again including Gavin, identified some kind of balance between the forces to result in the equilibrium situation of the load on the bridge, 'so there is an equal push down and up'.

Our evaluation indicated that there seemed to be an aspect of the bridge-building project that switched the students on to a scientific understanding of forces. One factor that made the project different from traditional, introductory physics courses was its hands-on nature. The students were constantly handling and testing the materials as they constructed the bridges and tested the consequences of putting a load on the bridge. Another student, James, discussed the 'tension in the wood' and this close feeling for the materials may have been a contributing factor in the students' understanding of the forces in action.

Aside from the practical aspects of the bridge project, the students were involved in complex problem solving. They were required to find their own solutions, for example, about how to increase the strength of their bridge while keeping costs to a minimum. This engaged the students in thinking about the materials available and their properties because they had to make decisions about their bridge based on this knowledge. The tests the students did with beams and structures at the beginning of the course played a significant part in their decision-making process. The tests often were mentioned by students as a way in which they found the solutions to their problems.

For example, Gavin and Colby found from their testing that 'I' beams were strong and the triangles were expensive, so they used 'I' beams for their bridge. Students were encouraged to be creative, and the prize for the most aesthetically pleasing bridge created an alternative dimension to the bridge-building project that complicated the process of problem solving. The students not only had to find solutions for the problems they encountered, the solutions had to be within parameters for strength, cost and aesthetics. This engaged the students in complex cost–benefit analysis.

The social, teamwork aspects of the bridge project were apparent. Students within groups worked together to test materials and conferred with each other to make decisions about their bridge. The structure of the project itself may have contributed to the students' understanding of forces. Students were introduced to ideas about static and dynamic forces early in the project, and the practical and social aspects of the course were likely to have reinforced those ideas. Another important aspect of this project was the content knowledge of the teacher. Ms O'Reilly had a background as an architect with a keen interest in engineering science. Her content knowledge was outstanding and this in itself may have been an important factor in the success of the integrated project.

In contrast with the encouraging results discussed above, there were indications that some of the students held misconceptions. One student, Lawrence, said that the load was the force acting on the bridge, which suggested that he saw a force as a property of a single object (the load) rather than an interaction between two objects. Other students' discussions indicated that they had an anthropomorphic view similar to that described by Viennot and Rozier (1994), where students saw a mass suspended from a spring 'as a dynamic conflict between the two objects in which the strongest of them determines a global motion in the direction of its own effort' (p. 239).

Although some of the students interviewed demonstrated robust understanding of the scientific principles associated with the bridge project, three of the five students interviewed did not think their scientific knowledge was useful during this project and one other student identified creativity as the only aspect of science that he used. For example, Steven discussed several ways in which he used his mathematics knowledge during the project, but said 'I don't think we did as much science'. Not only was there considerable science about forces embedded in this project, students were involved in investigating different structures in a scientific way to help them make decisions about the kind of bridge they would make. Gavin was the only student who said that science was useful for helping him with the investigations. Adam recognized that he was doing 'research' when he did the investigations, which he said that he liked, but he did not associate the investigations with science: 'I don't think [science was useful] so much for this project, but for some of the other projects'. One possible explanation for this lack of recognition of the science aspects of the technology project is that the students saw science more as a content-oriented subject rather than a skill or process-oriented subject. Most of the students recognized the process of doing mathematics; however, few students recognized when they were doing and learning science.

Issues-based approaches: A case study of the Wonthella Wetlands project

Hodson (2003) recommended radical change in the way that science curricula are structured, for two reasons: first, because science curricula no longer meet the needs, interests and aspirations of young people, and second because it is time for a science curriculum that supports socio-political action in order to solve current social and environmental problems. Hodson advocated a 'politicized, issues-based curriculum focused on seven areas of concern' (p. 645) comprising: human health; food and agriculture; land, water and mineral resources; energy resources and consumption; industry; information transfer and transportation; and ethics and social responsibility. According to Hodson, these seven areas of concern should be addressed at four levels of sophistication culminating in preparation for socio-political action (similar to Habermas's critical interest in Chapter 3).

Johnson (2004) pointed out the irony that while the most fundamental purpose of education is to build a citizenry prepared to work towards achieving prosperous, resilient and just communities, students and teachers frequently invoke the notion that, once out of school, the educated must learn to function in the 'real world'. Johnson argued that education should provide students with experiences that are genuine enough for them to learn practical ways to become good citizens. More specifically, Johnson said that the challenge for teachers of biology is to immerse students in situations that will foster the skills and desires to become 'stalwart caregivers of the Earth and its inhabitants, both human and nonhuman' (p. 550).

Ravetz (2005) claimed that the growing realization, since the 1960s, that our industrial civilization is unsustainable, that we are polluting ourselves and exhausting key resources, has changed our perception of reality. This change, according to Ravetz, is a revolution in thinking, somewhat akin to the Copernican revolution or the revolution of Charles Darwin's Theory of Evolution by Natural Selection. This notion of a 'paradigm shift' is also reflected in the writings of Capra (e.g., 1982) who claimed that 'we live today in a globally interconnected world, in which biological, psychological, social, and environmental phenomena are all interdependent' and that 'the holistic conception of reality, [is] likely to dominate the present decade' (Capra, 1996, p. xviii). We have noted previously that a common thread in many integrated programmes in schools is that they have connections with the environment in some way (Wallace *et al.*, 2007). In the following paragraphs we expand upon our findings from the case study at Kentish Middle School, where the teachers and students embraced environmental sustainability as an important issue around which to develop their entire curriculum.

The case study focused on a 10-week project that aimed to promote scientific literacy in the school and the community. In this context, scientific literacy was understood to mean using science-content knowledge and the findings from the project to make decisions about the ecological health and wellbeing of the wetland and understand how those decisions involved social and civic responsibility. Teachers at Kentish selected the project topic, 'Nutrification in the Wonthella Wetlands', because of the frequency with which the students used the wetlands for recreation. Teachers felt that there was opportunity for students to make a difference to the quality of the water in the local wetlands. One teacher, Mr Keane, commented: 'I like the idea of an 11-year-old being able to change the world, even just their own little bit of the world'.

It became evident during our observations at Kentish that there was a shift from the original focus on the nutrients in the wetlands onto broader issues. Each class within the learning community took a different project focus. For example, one class concentrated on the wetlands itself, another focused on houses and what people can do in their homes to contribute to the health of the wetlands, and another class looked at gardens and approaches to gardening that are environmentally friendly. The sequence of lessons was designed specifically to encapsulate problems associated with the wetlands, and assessment tasks were individualized and integrated.

Student outcomes

A survey administered prior to the project showed that Kentish students' knowledge of the wetlands was mostly related to the living things found there, such as ducks and kangaroos; personal family uses of the environment, such as bushwalking and picnics; and some knowledge of the physical environment, such as the jetty and playground. During the course of the project, the total number of ideas represented in the students' responses increased from 170 to 307 (Venville et al., 2008). The pattern of ideas also changed; for example, prior to the project only four ideas (2 per cent of ideas) evident in the students' responses related to factors impacting on the health of the wetlands. After the project this percentage increased, with 98 ideas (32 per cent) relating to factors about the health of the wetlands, including pollution, phosphates and salinity. Moreover, prior to the project, students offered only three ideas that referred to public responsibility for the wetlands, but after the project there were 25 ideas relating to responsibilities such as recycling and preventing domestic animals from going into the wetlands environment.

Interviews prior to the project supported the assertion that students tended to look at the wetlands from a personal perspective, with stories and anecdotes relating to picnics, barbecues and parties. After the project, when students were asked what they had learnt about the wetlands, the focus was not always on nutrients, but more on the broader topic of human impact on the health of the wetlands, with stories about pollution, salinity and habitat destruction.

Further, they were able to relate their personal experiences, the environmental consequences and potential solutions. For example, prior to the project, Andrew talked about his personal experiences at the wetlands:

> I think when I was young we went down there [to the wetlands] just to have a picnic. Or maybe once we went down there and we played a bit of cricket and football, because we were going down to have a barbecue there.

After the project, Andrew made the link between human activities, such as picnics and walking the dog and the associated litter, with environmental problems in the wetlands, such as excess nutrients. He also gave explanations of how pollutants get into the wetlands, and acid rain, and he remembered how he learnt about these ideas through a classroom modelling activity. During the post-project interview, Andrew also spoke of his experience of designing an 'eco-smart' house during the project, detailing how the excursions and activities in the class helped him to design his house and make an oral presentation.

Prior to instruction, Kurt thought about the wetlands in terms of picnics and some of the things he had observed during his visits there. In the post-instruction interview, Kurt was able to talk about the wetlands in terms of algal blooms, salinity, erosion and sustainable housing surrounding the wetlands. Below is an extract from his interview that demonstrates his conversation and knowledge about salinity.

Interviewer:	Okay, and what's this about salt here [referring to Kurt's post-project mind map]. What do you know about salt?
Kurt:	Um like, salt, can, when like the ground water has salt in it down below us now. There's salt in the ground, and when the ground water rises, the salt comes out. And like causes tons of salt on the land. When the water disappears from like, evaporation.
Interviewer:	And what does that do. Is that a good thing or a bad thing?
Kurt:	Bad thing.
Interviewer:	Why is that a bad thing?
Kurt:	Because the salt affects like the grass and everything. And kills the grass, and then the more and more ground water comes up. Since the trees are like, more salt resistant, they can keep the ground water safe, and like, the short-rooted ferns and everything can't. So yeah, they'll die.
Interviewer:	So how did you learn about that?
Kurt:	Um, we were doing, like, society and environment. We were doing things about, like, to make it healthy around the wetlands. We had to like, put stuff up we think is good

around the wetlands. So I put a car park away from the wetlands with trees around it. And a nature reserve, just in case like, animals get hurt in the car park so they can go to the nature reserve, and everything.

Interviewer: All right. Why did you put all the trees around the wetlands?

Kurt: Because they would keep the salinity down.

Through lessons in society and environment, Kurt was also able to transfer some of the ideas he had learned about the wetlands in science to other contexts such as surfing at a local beach.

> When you have a lot of fun near the water, it could actually destroy the water as well. So yeah, we did like an experiment on that in science. And we did something in society and environment. We had to like draw a grid up. And when fun causes pollution, like if we were doing surfing, you could damage the coral and everything. And if you were doing hang-gliding, parachuting off a boat, like when the boat pulls you along, the fuel and everything can go in the water.
>
> (Kurt, post-project interview)

Approach to assessment

Mr Keane explained that the approach to assessment in this learning community was different from the traditional approach of testing and examinations. The teachers collected data about the students' achievement in science in a more incidental and holistic way, so that by the end of the teaching term they had a number of pieces of evidence that allowed them to provide feedback to parents. This approach was consistent with the local curriculum documents that specified that teachers were to use criterion-referenced assessment in levels.

Mr Keane explained how this method of assessment was applied during a role play activity that was used by the teachers for assessment in three learning areas, including science, society and environment and English.

> The first is a role-play. Again, think of this as an assessment for English, science and society and environment. It's a role play in a scenario where a lake, not unlike Wonthella Wetlands, and there's a development planned for the northern side of the lake. They have to role play [stakeholders] in groups of five, one as developer, ... The Wonthella sailing club, ... the friends of the lake, ... And we can draw out the application of ideas from a science idea. From the science idea we have to apply to a social situation, but using English skills to do it. So this, and I think the discretion [between subjects] in that task disappears.
>
> (Mr Keane, post-instruction interview)

The civic nature of the outcomes from the project was clearly described by Mr Keane in the following excerpt from the post-instruction interview transcript:

> They've just changed their attitudes. They're not reactive anymore. They're actually active. They are actively making decisions and changing their world. They need to have that sort of personal power, and in a way, on a global scale, they're empowered.
>
> (Mr Keane, post-project interview)

The status of knowledge

In this section of the chapter we explore schemes for evaluating the status of knowledge and consider the appropriateness of these schemes with respect to integrated curricula. We use the two case studies described in the previous section to exemplify our assertions. Finally, we raise three questions: What is 'powerful knowledge' for students? What knowledge counts? How can such knowledge best be represented in curriculum documents so that students can readily have access to it?

Classification and frame

Bernstein (1971) created a typology that categorized subjects on the basis of whether the knowledge within the subject is highly differentiated from other subjects and the degree to which the content to be taught is tightly prescribed. We noted in Chapter 3 that Bernstein (1971, 2000) used the concepts 'classification' and 'frame' to describe the underlying structure of curriculum. By classification he referred to the nature of the differentiation of the content of one subject compared with others. Where classification is strong, the content of the subject is well insulated from the content of other subjects by strong boundaries. Where classification is weak, there is reduced insulation of content and the boundaries of the subject are weak or blurred. 'Classification thus refers to the degree of boundary maintenance between contents', wrote Bernstein (1971, p. 49). The contents of school subjects such as physics, history and literature, for example, are well differentiated from each other and, therefore, these subjects are strongly classified. In contrast, the content of a subject like environmental science is more weakly classified, because the boundaries between this subject and others, such as biology and geography, are less distinct.

Bernstein's (1971) concept of frame refers to the specific pedagogical relationship between the teacher and the pupil. Frame refers to the strength of the boundary between what may be taught and learned and what may not be taught and learned. Where framing is strong, there is a sharp boundary; where framing is weak, there is a blurred boundary between what may and may not be appropriate content. According to Bernstein (1971), 'frame refers to the degree of control teacher and student possess over the selection, organization and pacing of the knowledge transmitted and received in the pedagogical relationship' (p. 50). Although a subject like environmental science may be weakly classified, it still may be strongly framed if the content within it and how it is taught is tightly prescribed. If the teacher or the students may vary the content or the pedagogical activities to pursue a specific interest, for example, then the subject will be weakly framed. The idea of frame is closely associated with assessment. Where the content to be assessed is clearly described, the frame of the subject is strong; where the content to be assessed is not clearly described, the frame is weak. Through this analysis of classification and frame, Bernstein claimed that the highly classified and highly framed structures of the traditional secondary school subjects, such as chemistry and mathematics, provide for students who are university bound, but for those who are not, these subjects can be seen as meaningless.

The hierarchical nature of Bernstein's concepts of classification and frame have been extended and used by Parker (1994), de Brabander (2000) and Rennie (2007). Parker explained that the more strongly classified and strongly framed a subject is, the higher is its status. Conversely, weakly classified and weakly framed subjects have lower status. Subjects like physics and chemistry, therefore, have a high status because they are strongly framed and strongly classified, whereas a subject like environmental science is more likely to be weakly framed and weakly classified and have a lower status. A subject such as physical science, combining physics and chemistry, will be less strongly classified than either physics or chemistry, but may still be strongly framed. Its status would be intermediate between physics or chemistry and environmental science. Parker (1994) was able to demonstrate empirically the relationship between classification, framing and the status of science subjects in the Western Australian science curriculum. Likewise, Rennie (2007) found that when humanistic elements were incorporated into physics the course was considered to be of lower status by parents, students and teachers, and that this could be attributed to the weaker classification and frame of the course compared with a more classical, highly mathematics-based physics course.

de Brabander (2000), while investigating the conceptions or definitions of knowledge that teachers 'transmit', noted both the status differences and evidence of power differences between subcultures in secondary schools, including between school subjects. His findings suggested that teachers classified knowledge on two dimensions, firstly, as everyday knowledge or academic knowledge and secondly, as general or specialized knowledge. Subjects with everyday knowledge were considered 'soft'; that is, the knowledge they offer is not easily testable, it is subjective and relatively open to debate, as opposed to subjects providing 'hard' academic knowledge that is characterized as testable, objective and established. Art education and social studies were characterized as offering everyday knowledge whereas mathematics was viewed as the classical academic subject. Biology and Dutch language (the mother tongue in de Brabander's research) were considered 'in between'.

General subjects offer knowledge that is called for on many different occasions. Specialized subjects, on the other hand, offer knowledge that is only useful on infrequent, special occasions. Biology, physics and chemistry were clear examples of specialized knowledge and Dutch language was considered the most general subject.

The case studies revisited

Typologies, such as those presented by Bernstein and de Brabander, assisted us to critically analyse the status of the knowledge conveyed through a range of types of curricula that we investigated during our research programme. As a result, we have raised questions about the validity of the hegemony and pervasiveness of the disciplinary structure to school curriculum. Earlier in the chapter we described two cases where teachers and students were able to implement a different approach to curriculum, one where the structure of the curriculum was driven by the professional knowledge of engineers when bridge building, and one where the structure of the curriculum was driven by the need to address the environmental issues impacting on a local wetland. Here we consider these case studies, the status of the knowledge developed by the students when examined through the typologies from the literature, and question what is powerful knowledge for students in school in the twenty-first century.

The design brief for the bridge-building project at Southern High School underpinned the teaching and learning that occurred in the case study. Ms O'Reilly's background as a trained architect, with strong content knowledge in engineering, design and mathematics, meant that she was confident to draw on her knowledge in the teaching and learning of this project. The form of curriculum implemented in her classroom was consistent with that recommended by Rogers (1997), because the professional knowledge from engineering was used as an alternative to the disciplines as a source of authority for establishing a set of expectations and standards that the students used to construct and validate understanding. The bridge-building project had real-world relevance because it involved complicated problem solving with no easy or straightforward answers. Students worked as a team, and were required to carefully plan and manage their time. Students were involved in decision making about how to strengthen their bridge so that it met the strength standards, how to economize to meet the budget requirements, and how to design their bridge to make it aesthetically appealing. They were involved in multifaceted cost–benefit analyses, and used a combination of mathematical knowledge, science knowledge and design and technology knowledge to plan and build their bridge.

The environmental issues associated with the local wetlands were the driving force behind the curriculum observed in the learning community at Kentish Middle School. The findings from this case study clearly showed an increase in students' awareness of factors impacting on the health of the wetlands, and public responsibility for the wetlands environment. These were clearly representative of the core-shared values underpinning the curriculum, such as Social and Civic Responsibility and Environmental Responsibility (Curriculum Council of Western Australia, 1998). The subject-specific outcomes, while considered and utilized during planning by the teachers, were subordinate to the environmental issues. For example, the concept of the water cycle was used to help students understand environmental issues such as acid rain and the leaching of nutrients from garden fertilizers into the wetlands. The form of curriculum implemented in the learning community at Kentish Middle School was consistent with that recommended by Beane (1995), because the issues and problems surrounding the wetlands were the starting point rather than the subject-specific outcomes stated in the local curriculum documents (Curriculum Council of Western Australia, 1998). The approach to curriculum observed in the case study resulted from teachers shifting related ideas out of the subject matter content and working together on overlapping concepts, skills and attitudes. Concepts and processes from several learning areas of the state curriculum, in particular science, and society and environment, were used to inform and understand aspects of the central issue of the wellbeing of the wetlands. For example, teachers developed a programme that included the scientific process of testing the quality of the water of Wonthella Wetlands and made explicit links in society and environment to human activities, such as development and recreation.

If we consider the approaches to teaching and learning observed in these case studies from within the schemes proposed by Bernstein (1971, 2000) and de Brabander (2000), they can be considered to be weakly classified and weakly framed, everyday rather than academic, and general rather than specialized. Integrated topics, by their very nature, are weakly classified because their content is not well insulated from that of other subjects. The discourse from teachers and students presented in the findings, as well as evidence from classroom observations, clearly indicated that the projects were weakly classified.

In the bridge-building case study, the weak classification was evident in that the boundary between mathematics knowledge, science knowledge and design knowledge was not clear. One student was surprised when the teacher showed him how to work out how much the string for his bridge would cost using the proportional reasoning he often used in his mathematics class. The majority of students didn't realize that they were using scientific knowledge about forces, because they weren't learning science content and facts as such; rather, they were constructing a bridge and applying knowledge from multiple disciplines. The difference between learning science in the science classroom and learning science in order to apply it to building a model bridge may seem a subtle difference at one level, but it transforms the knowledge from being strongly to weakly classified, from being specialized knowledge to being general knowledge, and from being academic to being everyday.

In the wetlands case study, the content of the subject of science was not well insulated from the content of the subject of society and environment, and evidence presented in the case study indicated overlap with other learning areas including English, mathematics, art, and technology and enterprise. The teachers were explicit about their intention to blend the content from several subjects; indeed, this was observed and documented by the researchers at several levels during the wetlands project, including the planning, implementation and assessment levels.

According to Bernstein (1971, 2000), a school topic is weakly framed when there is not a strong boundary between what may be taught and learned and what may not be taught and learned. The content is varied and largely determined by the interests of the students and the teacher. The teaching and learning observed in the model bridge-building project can be considered to be weakly framed compared with what might be taught and learned in a traditional science or mathematics course. The teacher's background and expertise as an architect and the optional nature of the project resulted in a subject that was determined by the interests of the teacher and the students within this school context. Ms O'Reilly explained:

> Each year it changed and I tried things and if they worked we continued with them; if they didn't work we threw them out. We did a lot of negotiation with students. I found out what the students' interests were and we would follow that particular line of interest if we could.

While the teacher delivered a few lessons on the basics of design strength, the students were free to develop their own scientific tests to determine which strength structures they would incorporate into their bridge. The bridge design was not pre-determined and there were no instructions on how to construct the bridge; rather, students were encouraged to use their knowledge, the results of their tests and their creativity to develop their own unique model bridge within given parameters. The main outcomes of the project, as explained by the teacher, were very much focused on skills that would be expected in the profession of engineering, such as problem solving, critical thinking, analytical thinking, time management and teamwork.

The assessment in the bridge-building project also was not traditional. There was no test of the concepts learned during the course. Alternatively, students' model bridges were subjected to the same assessment criteria that real bridges would be subject to: strength, here tested by adding cartons of soft drink; aesthetic appeal, tested by the school's English head of department; and economy, tested by the degree to which students were able to stay within their budget. The approach to assessment liberated students from tasks that might be expected in a more traditional approach to physics, for example, such as memorizing formulae and pencil-and-paper problem solving. These factors contributed to the weakly framed nature of the project because what was taught and learned varied according to the idiosyncratic pathway groups of students took to the design and construction of their model bridges.

The findings from the urban wetlands case study indicated that the teachers and the students themselves often determined the direction of the student learning. Moreover, the assessment was structured around levels of understanding rather than a test of specified content knowledge. As in the bridge-building project, this approach to assessment enabled the students, and the five teachers, to pursue content areas of interest. For example, each teacher took responsibility for a smaller group of students within the learning community and created a different environmental focus for that group. Two of the observed groups of students selected the water cycle as the focus of their presentation, while other groups selected different science concepts including native vegetation, animal habitats and ecologically friendly houses.

Some students, like Andrew, understood concepts such as the water cycle and acid rain that were closely associated with the original topic of nutrients in the wetlands. Other students, like Kurt, had a relatively sophisticated understanding of the problem of rising salinity, and still others could explain the process of habitat destruction that is only loosely associated with the original focus of the topic. The differences in the content of the students' learning, however, did not have consequences, because the students could demonstrate levels of understanding in the context of their choice. Comments from Mr Keane about the structure of the assessments clearly indicated that it was the skills, the arguments, the ability to communicate, and the application of scientific concepts in social contexts that were important goals of the teaching and learning process in this learning community. The topic observed in this case study was weakly framed because there were blurred boundaries between what was taught and learned and what was not taught and learned.

The kind of learning observed in both case studies could also be considered to be 'soft', that is, difficult to test in an objective way. The content was subjective and relatively open to debate, in contrast with the 'hard' content knowledge found in subjects such as physics and calculus (de Brabander, 2000). In the model bridge project the students actively pursued different approaches to building their bridge, there was no 'correct' approach. In the wetlands project, the findings showed that all students in the learning community actively participated in a role play of community members debating the very issues about the wetlands that they had been learning. In both case studies, the absence of high-stakes testing enabled a broad spectrum of content to be considered at inconsistent depths by different students and resulted in a broad spectrum of innovative teaching strategies including role play, excursions, games, individualized projects and guest speakers. In the bridge-building project, the teacher claimed that her teaching approach enabled her to be 'facilitating the knowledge gain. They get their own knowledge, and some don't see that I am actually pulling!' The teachers in the wetlands project justified these approaches, claiming that the students 'need stimulation' and that the approaches helped students to 'respond', gave them 'ownership', made them 'empowered', 'connected to their own world', 'changed their attitudes', and, finally, resulted in them 'actively making decisions and changing their world'.

Conclusion

According to Parker (1994), weak classification and weak frame point to a low status for the topics taught in the two case studies. Low-status subjects are considered to contain content that is perceived as less worthwhile than others (Parker, 1994). Does this mean that the way that these topics were taught has resulted in the participating students being denied 'powerful knowledge' as described by Young (2008)? Young suggested that Bernstein's analysis of the structure of educational knowledge provides a way of 'explaining why, for example, students will learn little mathematics or science from a curriculum that relies largely on "street" or everyday examples of number use' (p. 21). Is this what we have observed in these case studies? Did the students learn little science, or non-powerful science, because the curriculum relied on close connection between student learning and a community issue and was driven by the values of environmental responsibility and social and civic responsibility in the wetlands project? Or does it mean that the students involved in the bridge-building project learnt little science or mathematics knowledge, or non-powerful knowledge, because the curriculum was based around a real-world profession such as engineering? We think not.

The factors that are considered to render the curricula in the two case studies as weakly classified and weakly framed, such as the close association between the science and society and environment concepts and the English skills of communication, are the same factors that also indicate the power for students of this approach to teaching and learning. Ms O'Reilly explained: 'In the evaluation over the years, the kids will always realize the team work and time management are extremely important aspects of it'. Mr Keane articulated, 'I can see these kids are going to be the kids that can explain why you shouldn't feed bread to the ducks down at the wetlands, and they actually have the science behind them. And from English they'll have the speaking and listening skills to actually deliver in that way'. The power of the knowledge taught and learned during the case studies is that it provided the students with skills in social and civic responsibility, power to think in ways that are appropriate to the problems and issues that face the community in which they live and the professions that they may one day pursue. It gave students the power to communicate and debate issues, power to think about ways that problems and issues can be solved, power to analyse and to think critically; in short, it provided students with knowledge that counts.

In this chapter we demonstrated how the integrated projects at Southern and Kentish incorporated knowledge from several disciplines to solve problems not only related to their specific project but also connected to real-world issues and how they are dealt with in society. We suggest that the teaching and learning observed in these cases can be described in different ways to those suggested by Young (2008) and Bernstein (1971, 2000). We find ourselves more in agreement with commentators such as Kelly *et al.* (2008), for example, who claimed that learning knowledge involves critical dispositions as learners participate in the discourse and actions of a collective social field. Likewise, Duschl (2008), in the context of science education, argued that learning goes beyond the conceptual and cognitive, and involves the social processes and contexts that shape how knowledge is communicated, argued and debated. In the chapter that follows, we take these ideas to another level, by arguing that the best kinds of integrated teaching and learning involve a constructive balance between discipline knowledge and integrated knowledge and connect local problems with global issues.

6 Knowledge that counts in a global community

Balance and connection

In the preface to this volume, we argued that 'Ours is a connected world. No event or issue is isolated from every other. What happens anywhere in the world can effect each of us'. Further, we noted that there are repercussions from this connectedness and in Chapter 1 we discussed the challenge of aligning our students' education with their future needs. The purpose of this chapter is to draw together the issues that we discussed in the previous chapters and the knowledge we developed through our extensive research programme on curriculum, and to look ahead to how we can help to provide our students with knowledge that counts in a global community.

The argument we present in this chapter is that a curriculum that will lead to a powerful education is one that balances disciplinary and integrated knowledge and one that connects global and local views. We introduced this approach in Chapter 3, naming it a Worldly Perspective for curriculum. We demonstrate that the balance and connection we advocate are intimately entwined, and that these two dimensions of curriculum can be used to critically examine the power of an enacted curriculum. In order to develop this argument, in the first section of this chapter we re-examine the issues of knowledge and power and problematize knowledge that counts in our global educational community. In the second section we offer the Worldly Perspective as an alternative to current models used for evaluating curricula. We describe two dimensions of the Worldly Perspective, the knowledge dimension and the locality dimension. In the third section of the chapter we draw on the dimensions of the Worldly Perspective to examine two vignettes of cutting-edge research to demonstrate how the Worldly Perspective can be used to evaluate and comment on knowledge and the utility and power of that knowledge. In the fourth section we look at the practicalities of a school classroom through a case study of students learning ecology, and see how the dimensions of the Worldly Perspective can be used to inform and critique an enacted curriculum. Finally, we advocate the use of the Worldly Perspective as an innovative way to evaluate the power of a curriculum with regard to the knowledge and skills it generates within students.

Knowledge that counts

As was discussed in earlier chapters, one of the major difficulties when implementing an integrated curriculum is that parents, teachers and, to a lesser extent, students become concerned that what is being taught and learned has a lower status, is less rigorous and less powerful than the content of disciplinary-based courses and subjects. This concern is reflected in the literature. For example, Young (2008) claimed that if knowledge transmission between generations is a key role of schooling, then some types of knowledge must be considered more worthwhile than others. In turn, the worthiness of knowledge must be the basis of the difference between school knowledge and non-school knowledge. He argued that the knowledge that takes people beyond their experience has historically been expressed largely in the disciplinary or subject forms.

Young (2008) expressed concern that the recent trend towards more choice and reduction in subject-specific content, while more engaging and relevant to students' contexts, inevitably disadvantages students, particularly those from socially and economically disadvantaged families. He argued that if schooling tries to modify the curriculum to be more consistent with the culture of the students, then it is failing in its role as an agent of cultural transmission. Young explained that powerful knowledge refers to what the knowledge can do, or what intellectual power it gives to those who have access to it. In a similar way, H. Gardner (2004) asserted that educators have to define as best they can the understandings that 'will count' (p. 234). Young pointed out that schools are not always successful in giving all students access to powerful knowledge, but that to deny the conditions for acquiring powerful knowledge is to do a disservice to students, particularly those who are already disadvantaged by their social circumstances.

Challenging assumptions about powerful knowledge

Kelly *et al.* (2008) argued that in many current education-based debates, there is an underlying assumption of a corpus of canonical, disciplinary, received wisdom that is beyond criticism. Further, these assumptions have been translated in curriculum documents into key criteria, standards or educational outcomes that are narrowly focused on what is readily measurable, or amenable to standardized achievement testing. Evidence to support this assertion is provided by Au (2007), who showed that the primary effect of high-stakes testing is that curricular content is narrowed to those subjects included in the tests, subject area knowledge is fragmented into test-related pieces, and teachers increase the use of teacher-centred pedagogies. Au concluded that high-stakes tests increase the control that policymakers have over what happens in schools and classrooms and this curricular control may contribute to educational inequality.

In the previous chapter we examined the case of a school that implemented an integrated, community-based science project that was underpinned by values such as social, civic and environmental responsibility, rather than the subject-specific objectives. There was evidence that students not only learned important science concepts, but they could relate these concepts to the environmental issues associated with a local wetland, and engage in critique and debate. The students' learning in science, however, was idiosyncratic and integrated with concepts from other subjects. The nature of the project, when viewed through frameworks developed by Bernstein (1971, 2000) and Young (2008), could be considered to result in students learning low-status, everyday and, therefore, non-powerful knowledge. These frameworks, however, did not seem to recognize the power of the integrated knowledge developed by the students. The power of the knowledge taught and learned during this case study was that it provided the students with skills in social and civic responsibility, power to think in ways that were appropriate to the problems and issues that faced the community in which they lived, power to communicate and debate these issues and power to think about ways that these problems and issues could be addressed. The case study clearly demonstrated that new ways of analysing the structure and status of knowledge are required.

A Worldly Perspective

In this section we develop in more detail our theoretical base for curriculum that we refer to as a Worldly Perspective. We first proposed this approach in 2002 (Venville *et al.*, 2002), and in Chapter 3 we re-introduced the Worldly Perspective and discussed its implications for student learning in integrated contexts. We also illustrated its use as a guide or referent for developing curricula using an integrated teaching framework. In this chapter, we develop in greater depth and provide more detail about what the Worldly Perspective looks like and how it might be used to make judgements about the power of the knowledge that a particular approach to curriculum may have for the participating students.

We propose a Worldly Perspective of curriculum that reflects a holistic view of knowledge, grounded in students' experiences, relationships and contexts. We argue that disciplinary knowledge is an important component of this holistic view. In fact, from a Worldly Perspective, it is necessary that the integrated paradigm and the disciplinary paradigm be considered together, overlapping rather than mutually exclusive. From a Worldly Perspective the disciplines are there, but they are omnipresent rather than omnipotent. Worldly knowledge draws from, but is not bounded by, the constraints of traditional disciplines and serves multiple curriculum interests. As Goodson (1992) pointed out, school subjects are blocks in the mosaic of the curriculum. We argue that the separation of integrated and disciplinary paradigms is artificial and does not describe the world as it is. A Worldly Perspective acknowledges high-status subjects such as literature, physics, history and chemistry but allows for these subjects to evolve within a broader framework than exists in most school contexts. This broader framework means that worldly knowledge is connected in some way to the experiences, contexts and needs of the students' school community, and that these local contexts need to be well connected with global communities, global ways of thinking and global ecologies.

The Worldly Perspective has two dimensions that can be used to evaluate the power of knowledge and learning that is likely to be developed through different approaches to curriculum. The first dimension is a knowledge dimension, examining the relationship between integrated and disciplinary ways of knowing. The second dimension is a locality dimension that includes issues and perspectives from local to global. In the following sections we elaborate each of these dimensions.

The knowledge dimension: Balancing discipline-based and integrated curriculum

In this section of the chapter we borrow the terms 'centripetal' and 'centrifugal' from Bakhtin's (1981) analysis of language to characterize the contrasting forces underlying integrated and disciplinary approaches to curriculum that form the first dimension of the Worldly Perspective for curriculum (see also Rennie *et al.*, 2011).

In terms of this metaphor, centripetal forces pull students inwards, towards a central unifying location within a particular discipline, such as science or history. This means that students are forced to look inwards, focusing on the orderliness of the discipline, with their learning maintaining both the content and practices of that discipline. The arguments behind this approach to curriculum flow from the notion that disciplines, such as history, provide specialized knowledge and ways of looking at the world that enable rigorous explanation of various phenomena. In this way, disciplines provide students with the skills and cognitive tools required to solve focused, discipline-based problems (Beane, 1995; Gardner and Boix-Mansilla, 1994; González, 2004; Schoenfeld, 2004). In opposition to centripetal forces, centrifugal forces push students outwards, towards diversity, disunity and multiplicity, and define learning and teaching in ways that are multifaceted (Leonardo, 2004). This outward-focused approach results in an integrated curriculum that disregards, or breaks down, strict disciplinary boundaries and enables teachers and students to participate in curriculum and instruction that respond to issues that may be more immediately relevant and motivating to young people and better reflect the realities of their experiences outside school.

We find this metaphor of centripetal and centrifugal forces useful for exploring the tensions between disciplinary and integrated approaches to curriculum, particularly with regard to how education researchers view learning. The looking-inward, looking-outward nature of this metaphor avoids the pitfalls of metaphors that put these curricular approaches at the opposite ends of a continuum or in mutually exclusive camps (for example, Fogarty, 2002). The metaphor enables us to visualize tension between the opposing forces and, more importantly, provides the possibility of a place where balance between these forces can exist and be represented. It also draws attention to the importance of theoretical frameworks in looking at the outcomes of curricula, because an exploration of learning outcomes in terms of the inwardly focused, discipline-based curriculum requires a different theoretical lens than does an exploration of learning outcomes in terms of the outwardly focused, integrated curriculum.

The locality dimension: Connecting local and global

The term 'global education' appears increasingly in formal curricula around the world. Mundy, Manion, Masemann and Haggerty (2007) explained that global educators advocate incorporating a large number of global themes or issues into the curriculum in an integrated fashion, using pedagogical innovation. Some years ago, Anderson (1977) defined global education as 'education for responsible citizen involvement and effective participation in global society' (p. 36). The key concepts associated with Anderson's definition were a new global scale and scope of human interdependence and membership, that students should understand their involvement in the global society, and the importance of making decisions and judgements and exercising influence. Further, Anderson explained that global education opposes education about 'other peoples' that creates a 'them/us' dichotomy and encourages nationalistic tendencies.

Case (1997) outlined a range of 'global topics' about which he believed people should be informed 'if their "worldview" is to expand beyond a *perspective on the local* (i.e., understanding solely the events and workings of one's own community or country) to a *perspective on the global* (i.e., understanding the events and workings of the world)' (p. 77, original emphasis). These topics included such things as cross-cultural awareness, global interconnections, global history and knowledge of alternatives or awareness of human alternatives. In essence, according to Case (1997, p. 77),

> students need to know that people across the world share some common values and differ in others, that events and forces in the world interconnect in powerful ways, that the world is facing a number of serious issues, and that these issues have deep historical roots and that humankind has the potential to alter the existing ways of 'doing business'.

Further, Case (1997) stated that global education should not be an occasional add-on that occurs within a designated global education unit. He argued that a global perspective should be 'infused throughout the curriculum' (p. 81).

In contrast with descriptions of global education, we find advocates for closely aligning students' education with their local environment, local issues and local community. For example, van Eijck and Roth (2010) described one movement: 'place-based education is an approach to schooling, where local settings become the integrating element in students' education' (p. 871), and 'place-based education is often defined as a teaching–learning process that centres on what is considered local – usually students' own "place", that is their immediate schoolyard, neighbourhood, town, or community' (p. 876). Examples of such integrated, place-based approaches to education are replete in the literature; sometimes they are recognized under the umbrella of the term place-based education, other times they are not.

The reasons for locating a child's education within their recognized locale or 'place' are strong. If we use environmental education as an example, it is clear that this topic deals with concepts and issues that are global, for example, ozone depletion and global warming. These concepts often are poorly understood by students (Gautier, Deutsch and Rebich, 2006) and it is difficult for students to make personal and local connections with these big and complex global concerns. They cannot readily observe the effects of global warming or ozone depletion and often they don't perceive that these issues will directly affect them or their families (Thomson and De Bortoli, 2008). Scepticism and action paralysis, that is, a feeling of not being able to make a difference, also may develop (Ballantyne, Connell and Fien, 2006). Many curricula seek to generate universal knowledge, abstract principles, theories and laws that can be applied to a number of contexts. Often it is the application of these principles, theories and laws that is missing in everyday classrooms and, as a consequence, school students do not recognize the relevance of science to their own lives, feel alienated and become disengaged (Cumming, 1996; Osborne, Simon and Collins, 2003).

Place-based education can be a way of implementing environmental education so that it brings school children closer to their natural environment and the problems and issues relevant to these environments. According to van Eijck and Roth (2010), 'place-based education is a counter-movement against those forms of science education in which students often lose their sense of place by focusing on global or abstract issues that bear no tangible relation to place' (p. 878). Gruenewald and Smith (2008) further question what they see as an underlying assumption that the purpose of school is to prepare students to compete and succeed in the global economy. They argue that, at its most fundamental, place-based education must overcome the isolation of school from the community and that 'the walls of the school must become more permeable' (p. xx).

Recent commentaries on place-based education recognized a problem with the use of the terminology: it does not readily allow or recognize that different people have different conceptualizations of 'place' depending on their worldview (Coughlin and Kirch, 2010). van Eijck and Roth (2010) explained that the word 'place' has emerged as problematic because we are in a world that we both share with others and experience in different, unique ways. Individuals can only see their place through their own ideology or worldview. These authors outlined a case study around Tod Inlet Marine Park, situated in the Pacific Coast region of British Columbia, Canada, that was made a Natural

Park during the 1990s. The case study outlines the differences in perspective from a western world view that supported many restoration and conservation activities and a First Nations, or W̱SÁNEĆ (Saanich), world view that expressed mixed feelings that this sacred place was taken deliberately and with intention and that the transition to Natural Park status locked the people out from traditional ways (van Eijck and Roth, 2010).

> Throughout our entire lives, we are embedded in a historical socio-cultural context in which we are acting and being acted upon by the world and other people. These relationships place us in a constant state of co-evolution with and from the processes of interaction. We cannot develop – or more fundamentally, exist – apart from our lived environments; human consciousness is predicated on the interaction between people and the world.
>
> (Coughlin and Kirch, 2010, p. 916)

One of the core themes in place-based education suggested by Gruenewald and Smith (2008) is interdependence, or an education that acquaints students about how their own health and security are co-dependent on the health and security of everyone and everything around them. According to Gruenewald and Smith, this interdependence is not abstract and is best understood by the study of relationships and systems including natural systems, cultural systems and civic associations.

We recognize both connection and tension between what we have described above as the 'global' view of education and a 'place-based' or 'local' view of education. On the one hand, it seems that commentators from each of the perspectives argue for completely different things, education that embraces the global versus education that embraces the local. On the other hand, commentators for both perspectives appeal to concepts such as 'interconnectedness', 'environment', 'systems', 'cultural awareness' and 'advocacy'. Both perspectives argue the importance of students understanding their interconnectedness to other people and to natural systems and to communities. The difference is simply the location and scope of the systems and communities. Further, both perspectives argue against the homogenization of culture under globalization (Gruenewald, 2003). We strongly support the notion that the connection and interaction between people and the world cannot be ignored in school curricula.

Bringing the dimensions together

While both these dimensions conjure images of a continuum, we remain true to our previous argument that notions of a continuum are not helpful in considering knowledge or curriculum because they suggest that movement along a continuum is movement towards a better or more powerful state. Rather, we propose that the power of the curriculum is indicated by the degree to which a curriculum promotes balance between integrated and disciplinary perspectives of knowledge (the knowledge dimension) and the degree to which a curriculum promotes connection between local and global perspectives (the locality dimension). In order to provide context for our argument that balance and connection provide the key to powerful knowledge, we present two vignettes of award-winning researchers and examine their work through the knowledge and locality dimensions of the Worldly Perspective.

Vignette 1: Conservation and computer modelling

The Australian 2010 Scopus Young Researcher of the Year in the Life Sciences and Biological Sciences category was University of Adelaide researcher Corey Bradshaw, a mathematical ecologist. One aspect of Bradshaw's work was the development of a computer model to test scenarios in a virtual Kakadu National Park (located in the Northern Territory of Australia) to establish the cheapest and best culling programmes to limit the damage from pests such as feral buffalo, horses and pigs ('Conservation', 2010). Corey Bradshaw said to *The Australian* newspaper's Higher Education Supplement, 'I realized the best thing I could do for my career was to get adept at mathematics' (p. 24). He further explained that 'mathematics is a fundamental component of all biology now, especially ecology, because it's such complex systems we're dealing with' (p. 24). Bradshaw's model divides the Kakadu landscape into a grid and equations are used to consider data from field studies, such as the number of breeding females and birth and mortality rates. Prior to the work in Kakadu, Bradshaw's team analysed the critically endangered grey nurse shark species and found the biggest threat was fishing; not beach nets or a lack of protected areas as previously thought. Bradshaw explained to the Higher Education Supplement that the findings have influenced conservation policy.

Why is the knowledge that Corey Bradshaw developed award winning? If we examine the research that he does from the two dimensions of the Worldly Perspective the answer to this question becomes evident. From the knowledge dimension, Bradshaw's work draws from a number of disciplines to address the issues of feral and endangered species. While these issues sit clearly within the broad discipline of biology, Bradshaw's work draws on concepts and principles from the sub-disciplines of conservation biology, genetics and ecology, and from the alternative disciplines of mathematics and computer modelling. The work is, therefore, not based within a single discipline. As Bradshaw explained, however, his depth of knowledge in the single discipline of mathematics was the key to the promotion of his career and the award-winning nature of his research. From the knowledge dimension, we can see balance between discipline-based and integrated perspectives of knowledge in Bradshaw's work, where both are utilized and brought to bear on the issues at hand.

From the perspective of the locality dimension, Bradshaw's work in Kakadu National Park is very much a local issue related to feral animals destroying the natural landscape and habitats of indigenous species in that very localized part of the world. The issue of feral animals and the destruction of natural habitat are, however, global issues faced in all continents and countries on our planet. The work Bradshaw did with the grey nurse shark also is focused, in that it examines a population problem for one particular marine species. Again, the issue of endangered species is a global issue and the mathematical processes and techniques he developed are globally applicable. We argue that the connection between the local and the global in Corey Bradshaw's work is strong and powerful.

Do we want young people to grow up to be able to think and work like Bradshaw? Do we want curricula that help young people to balance disciplinary and integrated knowledge and be able to make connections between global and local issues in the way that Bradshaw is able to do? We think the answer to these questions is a resounding 'yes', because this is how cutting-edge knowledge producers today develop powerful knowledge, and it indicates the nature of knowledge that counts in the world of the future. The balance between discipline-based and integrated knowledge and the connection between local and global are very powerful modes of thinking and working that are clearly demonstrated in Bradshaw's work. Ideally, we would like to see school curricula of the future being able to capture the kind of knowledge that this story epitomizes. The two dimensions of the Worldly Perspective and the notions of balance and connection potentially provide a framework through which such curricula might be evaluated.

Vignette 2: Bone analysis techniques for crime scenes

Daniel Franklin, a physical anthropologist at the University of Western Australia, was interviewed by *The Australian* newspaper about his innovative approach to forensic science using anthropological knowledge of bones (Rowbotham, 2010). Franklin explained that the great advances in the study of bones have hardly been applied to forensic science, even though 'there is more recognition now that we can increase the chances of identifying unknown people using these methods' (p. 21). Franklin is working on research to enhance bone analysis as a forensic tool. His team will examine sophisticated computer programmes for 3-D imaging that can easily be understood by scientists, police and juries, and new techniques of chemical analysis that will reveal information such as nutrition, diet and regional habitat. Franklin also is of the view that the work is likely to help forensic identification in natural disasters, such as earthquakes and tsunamis (Rowbotham, 2010).

If we examine this story through the two dimensions of the Worldly Perspective, we can begin to understand why Franklin's work in forensics is considered innovative and powerful. Franklin is primarily an anthropologist, but his work involves chemistry, computer imaging, geometry, geography and dietetics. As a consequence, his work promotes balance between his in-depth knowledge of anthropology, in particular palaeo-anthropological studies, and the integrated knowledge from many disciplines that can be brought to bear on the identification of human remains. Identifying human remains in forensic science is very intimate and personal and, therefore, a local issue. But, at the same time, the issue has global importance, particularly in earthquakes and tsunamis, the natural disasters that Franklin mentions, when the identification of human remains can take on global proportions. The connection between local and global in this work is even more evident when the methods Franklin plans to use are considered. He will use bone samples from all over the world to develop a new set of references against which bones in forensic cases can be compared to establish information like sex, age and ethnicity which can assist in identification. Currently there are no Australian standards, so Franklin claims 'it's a novel undertaking, a human identification package' (Rowbotham, 2010, p. 21).

We argue that this second story also illustrates powerful ways of thinking and working in a cutting-edge field that epitomizes the way that we would like to see school curriculum developed. Franklin's work combines balance between specialized, discipline-based knowledge and integrated ways of putting the knowledge together, and strong connections between local relevance and global importance. We believe that if the theoretical and practical aspects of school curriculum reflect an appropriate combination of balance and connectedness, the outcomes can provide students with powerful knowledge.

The Worldly Perspective and the practicalities of the school curriculum

A Worldly Perspective provides a way of reconciling the apparent antagonism between the proponents and opponents of curriculum integration and the issues around global and local approaches to education. We recognize that a curriculum structure based around school subjects is well supported by the long-established routines, structures and hierarchies of schooling, and we understand that a Worldly Perspective may present some challenge to these routines, structures and hierarchies. We noted earlier that Tylack and Tobin (1994) referred to these deeply entrenched routines as the 'grammar of schooling' and explained that they present barriers to educational change in general. The Worldly Perspective utilizes the academic disciplines but places those disciplines within a holistic, more organic view of knowledge. This perspective also acknowledges the global and local aspects of education and the interconnections in our rapidly changing world. This view resonates with the suggestion by Hirst and Peters (1970) that practitioners focus on developing students' knowledge and experiences that are both independent and yet intimately interrelated. We argue that the success of a Worldly Perspective approach to curriculum depends on the degree of balance between disciplinary and cross-disciplinary vision and on the connection between global and local applications and considerations.

In the next section we revisit and expand upon our case study of Brampton High School and examine the impact of the school context on the process of implementing an integrated curriculum. We then reflect on the case study from the two dimensions of the Worldly Perspective and speculate about the power of the knowledge developed through this curriculum for the participating students.

School case study: Brampton High School

Brampton High School was a traditional high school, located in a working-class outer suburb of a major city. The school was organized into subject departments and the classroom timetable revolved around the subjects. The focus of the case study was an academic extension class of Year 9 students who had been selected to be in this class on the basis of norm-referenced scores in school-based science topic tests. This case study included the 26 students in the class, the class science teacher, Ms Wills, and the academic extension coordinator, Mr Johnson. We previously analysed this case study of an integrated curriculum using the frameworks of Bernstein (1971, 2000) and Young (2008), and the full analysis and findings can be found in Venville *et al.* (2008). Here we re-analyse the case study and the complexities presented in a real classroom context from the perspectives of the two dimensions of the Worldly Perspective.

Implementation of the project

The 10-week project at Brampton was implemented in four 55-minute science lessons per week. Students remained with this class for all subjects and studied science in a school laboratory that was equipped with standard school science resources. Mr Johnson believed that this class had the academic ability to cope with the demands of such a project and believed that there was suffi-cient flexibility in the class timetable to schedule field trips. The chosen topic was 'Midge in the Local Environment'. ('Midge' is the common name used for the adult form of a small, mosquito-like insect.) This was considered an appro-priate topic by Mr Johnson and Ms Wills because of the problem that midge populations caused the students in their out-of-school activities such as sport and recreation. 'This is a real problem and there are kids in the class who have midge as a problem at home, which affects them and their parents in different ways' (Ms Wills, post-project interview). Although this was the only class participating in the midge project, all other Year 9 classes (nine classes in total) were participating in an ecology unit and the assessments, including the end-of-topic test, were common to all students.

> It was linked directly to what they were doing, all of the Life and Living Year 9 ecology type work fitted in very well with this. It was virtually a whole term's worth of work we'd look at, ecology and ecosystems. ...

In terms of learning outcomes, yeah, it definitely hit very well with what we normally do.

(Mr Johnson, post-project interview)

The Year 9 academic extension teachers (mathematics, science, English, and society and environment) met early in the school term to discuss student progress and an attempt was made to determine whether the science-based midge project could be integrated into other subject areas.

I would like the other core areas to know what we are doing, perhaps maybe use some of the data, for example in maths, some of the research information in English and perhaps some of the history of Lake Wonthella or something in society and environment because they are actually doing Australian landforms.

(Ms Wills, pre-project interview)

Ms Wills initially hoped the teachers of the other subjects would consider the issue of the midge in a more global way:

Also you could look at problems that have occurred in other places, for example, I know they have used fish in other areas to control some sort of macro invertebrate problem. They [teachers in other learning areas] could look at investigating other sorts of problems and solutions, to look from a more global perspective, I suppose.

(Ms Wills, pre-project interview)

The subject teachers, however, claimed that the learning activities and assessments within their learning areas had already been planned. Consequently, the non-science subject teachers did not become involved in the project, leaving the prime responsibility for classroom implementation with the science teacher, Ms Wills.

Maths is always difficult to integrate with. And they want to do their own thing and that particular [maths] teacher's very much into her world and can't work outside there, and she's very traditional.

(Mr Johnson, post-project interview)

Further, the school timetable restricted the interaction of the teachers, the potential of the class to go on field trips, and the flexibility of blocks of extended time for investigations, research and visits from scientists (Venville *et al.*, 2008).

Ms Wills was a qualified secondary science teacher with strong pedagogical content knowledge in the biological sciences. She continued to use the common Year 9 syllabus that outlined content and skills to be taught in the ecology unit, but modified the approach so that the midge project could be applied to the ecology content. Ms Wills explained the relationship between the project and the ecology course: 'Well, I definitely wanted them to do some ecology before we got into the project. So getting into the project first up, because they don't do ecology in Year 8, was a little bit difficult' (Ms Wills, post-project interview). As the term progressed, Ms Wills found that, as she had anticipated, the students did not have the science skills and knowledge necessary to plan and conduct their own investigations of the midge problem in the region. As a result, she embarked on a series of formal science lessons designed to teach the students the necessary content and skills, such as basic ecological terminology, insect life cycles, food webs and food chains and the use of the binocular microscope. Students then applied their understandings of food webs to midge and related organisms and their knowledge of scientific drawings to draw midge structure and function.

Student outcomes

Survey and interview data indicated that students learnt a considerable amount during the project and their responses increased in complexity as a result of the learning tasks undertaken. Before the project, the students at Brampton provided written responses to the open-ended survey question 'What do you know about midge?' Prior to the project, 53 distinct ideas from the 26 students were evident (see Table 6.1). After the project, student responses were more prolific with 108 separate ideas documented. Table 6.1 shows that prior to

Table 6.1 Categories of ideas from students at Brampton High School about the question 'What do you know about midge?'

Category of idea	Pre-project survey ideas		Post-project survey ideas	
	n	*%*	*n*	*%*
Relating to environment (pond/lake)	13	25	12	11
Don't know	11	21	0	0
Relating to self/family/personal	11	21	20	19
Misconceptions about midge	7	13	5	4
Relating to students' environment	3	6	0	0
Relating to midge breeding, causes and control	3	6	37	35
Midge life cycle	0	0	15	14
Food chain, ecosystem	0	0	7	6
General comments	5	9	12	11
Totals	53	100	108	100

Note: *n* of students = 26.

the project many of the students (11 of 26 students) felt they didn't know anything about midge, but after the project none responded in this way. Pre-project responses from students with some knowledge of the midge usually related to their personal experiences (11 of 53 or 21 per cent of ideas) or to the lake environment where midge swarms are most populous (25 per cent). For example, Holly wrote: 'I have heard that they [midge] can get in your mouth and in your nose.' After the project, student responses to the survey question also included comments related to their personal experiences (20 of 108 or 19 per cent of ideas), but there were many more comments relating to midge life cycles (14 per cent), causes of swarms and methods of control (35 per cent), and some comments about food chains and the ecosystem (6 per cent). Holly's post-project response was: 'The adult midge lay eggs in the water then they evolve into larvae (still under water) then into pupa then out of the water into an adult. The adult midge survive for a max of 14 days'.

It was clear that students had improved their qualitative and quantitative understanding of the midge, its life-cycle, methods of control and how these organisms fitted into the ecosystem. During interviews prior to the project, most of the 10 students interviewed indicated they were aware of the midge by talking about their own personal experiences of the problem. For example, some students observed that midge live near the lake and are attracted to light. None mentioned life cycles or control of midge prior to the project. During post-project interviews, students demonstrated an increase in knowledge about the midge life cycles and control of midge. For example, all three students quoted below (Alex, Calia and Jess) mentioned the midge and the problem this causes for other organisms. Jess also mentioned the cause of the swarms being related to excess phosphorus in the water and phosphorus-feeding plants as another method of control of the midge.

> Well, where I live there's like heaps of midges around all the night, like the groups and stuff. ... And I think they're attracted to the light, 'cause they're always like, in our house near the light bulbs. And they live near the lake.
>
> (Alex, pre-project interview)

> Well, the reason some neighbourhoods are like being swarmed by them is because they live near a lake, and that's where the midge breed and live and stuff. The adult midge, they lay the eggs in the water, then they evolve into the larvae, and then in the water still, the pupa. Then it comes out, the pupa evolve into an adult, and um, then they're out of the water. And they come out in summer, when it's like humid and stuff. And during like the early evening. And they end up in houses because they are attracted to light. ... Some people are trying to solve this problem, and they do that by sometimes spraying chemicals over the lake to kill them off, but they

can't do it all the time because it affects other things as well around the lake.

(Alex, post-project interview)

Midges are always around water or like at least near water. They always like, every time I see them, they're always in big swarms and move together, and I think that they're attracted to light.

(Calia, pre-project interview)

Okay, well, I now know that there's four main stages in their like development. Um, the eggs and then the larvae and then the pupa and then they grow after that. They grow wings and then come out of the water. They don't bite. They feed on like decaying animals and um, anything that kind of falls down into the wetlands and they usually go around in big groups.

(Calia, post-project interview)

No, I haven't seen any swarm in my areas. I also don't know why they occur.

(Jess, pre-project interview)

Well what I did learn is that they're small, their general size is very small, and they can um, they can go through most houses by, even through fly wire. And how um, and what's causing an overdose of like, of midge is by the phosphorus entering the lake and that's feeding the bloodworms [midge larvae]. ... And there are solutions to that by planting the phosphorus-feeding plants around the lake. And, basically, that's pretty much it. [Interviewer: Okay. Anything else at all?] That, I do know that in time they'll eventually grow immune to some insecticides, and another problem is that they'll be destroying natural predators of the midge [by using chemicals].

(Jess, post-project interview)

It is evident from the excerpts presented above that while the interviews elicited more information from students; they generally reflected similar trends to the survey question about the changes in students' knowledge.

A Worldly Perspective on the case study findings

The knowledge dimension

If we examine the outcomes of the case study through the knowledge dimension of the Worldly Perspective, it is evident that the teaching and learning that occurred in the class at Brampton High School was closely aligned with the school subject of science and the real-world contextual issue of the midge in the local environment. The case study showed an enacted curriculum that was integrated because it reflected the realities of students' experiences outside school; that is, it connected with their prior knowledge and experiences of the midge in the local environment. Whether the implemented project promoted balance between a disciplinary approach and an integrated approach, however, is questionable as the science perspective was strong and other disciplinary perspectives on the midge problem were not addressed. During the pre-project interview, the teacher expressed a vision for greater integration with the teachers of other subjects contributing, for example, 'maybe use some of the data in maths', 'some of the history of Lake Wonthella', or 'Australian landforms' in society and environment. However, as the project unfolded these subjects continued to be taught separately, and there was very little integration between them. It is interesting that the common conceptual understandings between the science learning area and the society and environment learning area about the environment and natural systems were explicitly linked in the state curriculum, but even though the possibility was available, they were not explicitly linked during this project. While some newspaper articles were considered in science class and students did mention ideas about the fly wire used in homes, the students did not study the social implications of the midge swarms during society and environment lessons and the majority did not discuss or mention such perspectives in the survey question or the interviews. In this way, the curriculum in the class at Brampton High School could be described, at best, as multidisciplinary (see Chapter 2) because students were expected to make the connections with other learning areas themselves.

The discipline-based structure of the teaching departments at Brampton and the discipline-based qualifications and strong discipline-based affiliation of teachers at the school provided a barrier to the implementation of the integrated project at this school. The teacher involved in the project was biology trained. Her subject-based training and history of science-based teaching strategies and resources was an indication of the strong degree to which a disciplinary vision of knowledge was valued by individual teachers and subject departments. As a consequence, when an attempt was made to integrate science with other subjects for the purpose of the project, the pre-planned content and assessments in each subject worked against a more broadly integrated approach. The closed nature of the classroom (i.e., there was little interaction with teachers and/or students from other classes) and the common assessment tasks used across all Year 9 science classes meant that the teacher did not have the freedom to deviate substantially from a discipline-based approach to the curriculum. These aspects of the educational context of the classroom at Brampton suggested a curriculum philosophy that was focused on the specialization and depth of knowledge associated within traditional subjects such as science. The school and classroom contexts resulted in the teaching being focused on the concepts and processes of science, even though the explicit purpose of the project was to integrate. The project about midge was designed to 'fit in' as an example of the concepts that were part of the pre-planned ecology topic that was the driving force behind what students were taught. Ms Wills explained:

> It [the midge project] has fitted in because we talked about life cycles, we've talked about where they [midge] fit in the food webs and food chains and food pyramids, and we used midge as an example in that. … So you know, just bringing it in constantly, in little bits and pieces, while we do different things.
>
> (Ms Wills, post-project interview)

The content and processes of science as a subject were maintained and perpetuated throughout the project, with the focus on disciplinary, academic rigour.

The locality dimension

If we examine the outcomes of the case study through the locality dimension of the Worldly Perspective it can be seen that students did develop more global perspectives with regard to midge over the period of the project. Before the project, the students had very local, personal comments about the midge. They complained about the midge in their local environment and how the insects irritated them during recreational activities and when relaxing at home. After the project, students still mentioned their personal problems and experiences with midge but they were far more knowledgeable and could link their personal knowledge of midge with more global scientific understandings from their ecology topic such as insect life cycles, food chains, food webs and energy transfer. In the classroom, these ecological concepts were used to explain the problematic midge swarms in terms of increased nutrients in the lake resulting in increases in the population of the algae producers in the food chains and subsequent increases in the first-order consumers, or midge. These global scientific concepts are applicable to other species and other contexts. In this particular class at Brampton, however, explicit teaching of the global application of the scientific ideas was limited. Questions and issues such as whether midge were a problem in other communities within the same city or other cities, or whether there are similar swarm-related problems with other species of flying insects in other locations, were not considered.

We assert that from the locality dimension of the Worldly Perspective there was evidence of connection between global and local because the students applied global scientific concepts, such as food chain and energy transfer, to their own local environment and a local species of relevance to their own lives. However, the connection between global and local could have been further enhanced had the local issues of relevance been connected with more global issues, such as pollution from chemical insecticides and phosphorus from fertilizers. Alex conveyed an understanding in the post-project interview that 'spraying chemicals … affects other things around the lake', and Jess mentioned the idea that midge will 'grow immune to some insecticides'. The global issue of genetic resistance to insecticides could have been considered in more depth, and examples of other species in other contexts could have been examined to develop the connection between local and global issues to a greater degree. Further, the social and economic implications and the ethical concerns with regard to the use of chemical insecticides could have been explored. Importantly, Indigenous Australian perspectives about the ecology and human use of the wetlands area could have been compared and contrasted with the Western world views of the majority inhabitants.

In summary, the approach to curriculum at Brampton High School can be considered powerful because it gave students access to the discipline-based subject matter they needed to know to pass the common Year 9 test. The approach also gave the students access to global science concepts applied to a local relevant and important issue. In this sense, there was some balance between integrated and discipline-based knowledge and some connection between global and local. However, the students had limited access to broader, global perspectives that could have been introduced and developed by teachers with expertise in the other disciplines. Hence the enacted curriculum was lacking in power because it favoured a discipline-based approach and was not well balanced with an integrated approach. The enacted curriculum also was focused on the local example of the midge and only gave minimal consideration to global implications and examples. In the context of this school, the teacher can be commended for the degree of balance and connection achieved through the curriculum; however, this analysis has revealed how the incorporation of more powerful knowledge might be attempted.

Our exploration of the case study at Brampton High School from the two dimensions of the Worldly Perspective revealed the entwined nature of the knowledge dimension and the locality dimension. We observed that there is a relationship between the degree of balance between discipline and integrated approaches to curriculum and the degree of connection between local and global. We assert that a greater balance between discipline-based and integrated approaches enables a better connection between local and global views of the world.

Conclusion

In this chapter, we challenged the current frameworks used to make judgements about the status or power of knowledge developed through different curricula, in particular, the approach suggested by Young (2008), based on the theory of Bernstein (1971, 2000). We proposed the Worldly Perspective as an alternative way of examining knowledge and making judgements about the power of knowledge that a curriculum can have in today's global community. The Worldly Perspective consists of two dimensions, the knowledge dimension and the locality dimension. The better a curriculum demonstrates balance between discipline-based and integrated knowledge and the better it focuses on the connection between global and local issues, the more powerful the curriculum, and the more intellectual power it provides to those who have access to it. Intellectual power gained though balance and connection is more than taking a discipline-based approach, an integrated approach, a place-based or local approach, or a global approach. Balance and connection are the drivers of a curriculum that provides powerful knowledge, knowledge that counts in a global community.

7 A new understanding of curriculum integration
Using a Worldly Perspective

Throughout this book we have explored both the theory and practice of integrated curriculum to determine what it can contribute to the education of the child in the global world of the twenty-first century. The outcomes of our investigations, as we have shown, are complex and multilayered. In several places in the book we have referred to the notion of a Worldly Perspective. We first used the term 'Worldly Perspective' in a 2002 publication in *Studies in Science Education* (Venville *et al.*, 2002). This publication included a comprehensive review of the literature available at the time and drew on our experiences of examining a wide spectrum of teaching and learning contexts that involved integrated approaches to curriculum. An instrumental reason for our first use of the term was that we wished to avoid describing what we were observing in classrooms in terms of a continuum from discipline-based approaches to integrated approaches. What we observed was a multifaceted approach to curriculum integration, including elements of the teaching and learning of discipline-based content knowledge alongside, before, after, and sometimes in the middle of integrated concepts and ideas. We wanted to capture the wonderful complexities of what we were observing and write about the diverse approaches to teaching and learning that were described by the teachers as integrated, without excluding the disciplinary components of what we saw. It also became clear to us that a perspective broader than either a discipline-based or an integrated perspective was needed to understand the diversity of what we were observing.

As our research programme matured, we continued to elaborate and elucidate what we meant by a Worldly Perspective. We used it as a tool, a wide-angle lens perhaps, to capture the diversity of curriculum integration. We hope that this book illustrates how a Worldly Perspective can be used to view curriculum integration from an educational researcher's point of view. In this seventh, final chapter, we distil seven key features, or components, from the book that represent the essence of the Worldly Perspective. In the following paragraphs each of these key components is briefly explained and we refer to the book chapters where more detailed information and examples can be found. We have done this so that the richness of the Worldly Perspective is not lost in a brief explanation. While we have been able to isolate what we believe are the key components of the Worldly Perspective, we adhere to our assertion that teaching and learning are complex, multifaceted processes, and that this complexity must be embraced by teachers, educators and educational researchers.

1. The Worldly Perspective acknowledges multiple approaches to curriculum integration

There are multiple approaches to curriculum integration, some of which are identified and elaborated in Chapter 2. For example, we described and provided examples of a synchronized approach, a thematic approach and a project-based approach to curriculum integration, among others. Each of these approaches included the teaching and learning of disciplinary knowledge as well as knowledge that can be referred to as integrated. It is interesting, but not surprising, that in different schools and with different teachers and different students one single approach, such as a thematic approach, may look very different and may certainly include knowledge that can be described as either more or less integrated. We found that when the school context and the teachers' and students' needs and interests were taken into consideration, one approach to integrating curriculum in one school could not be considered better or worse than a different approach in another school. The different approaches were simply different. The Worldly Perspective acknowledges multiple approaches to curriculum integration and we encourage teachers and educational researchers to explore in depth the reasons why a certain approach within a particular educational context may be justified.

2. The Worldly Perspective recognizes factors that enable and inhibit implementation of an integrated curriculum

There is a multitude of factors that may enable or inhibit the implementation of an integrated curriculum. A disciplinary approach to structuring curriculum remains the status quo throughout the world and the majority of curriculum documents, school structures and conventions are geared towards enacting a curriculum that is focused on imparting and assessing discipline-based knowledge. Regardless of the integrated nature of most of the problems facing the human species and our Earth, implementing an integrated curriculum requires working against this status quo. In Chapter 3 we identified a number of factors that may enable the implementation of an integrated curriculum, factors which, when not present, may inhibit the implementation. Some of these factors include small and stable learning environments, visionary and supportive leadership, team activities linked to the classroom, in-school planning time, a flexible school timetable and community links. The Worldly Perspective recognizes these contextual factors, and we encourage teachers and educational researchers to determine the extent to which these factors may or may not be present in particular educational contexts and hence influence the outcomes of an integrated curriculum.

3. The Worldly Perspective recognizes different curriculum interests and advocates for a balance among those interests

In Chapter 3 we explored various types of goals for the teaching of an integrated curriculum through the notion of 'interests' as described by Habermas (1971). The Worldly Perspective recognizes the legitimacy of different interests. For example, the technical interest in curriculum integration refers to the need for students to come to a better understanding of the disciplinary techniques, ideas and concepts behind a topic. The practical interest refers to the manner in which students make personal sense of the integrated topic being studied, how they solve problems and communicate their ideas. The critical interest involves students questioning current practices, considering how those practices may be changed, and taking personal or political action to achieve changes to the status quo. The Worldly Perspective favours a curriculum framework that incorporates a balance among these interests; technical, practical as well as critical.

4. The Worldly Perspective acknowledges the importance of multiple arguments for curriculum integration

The big question, 'Why use a particular approach to curriculum?', should be answered with reference to the expected learning outcomes. In Chapter 4 we outlined three arguments that might be used to support an integrated approach to curriculum. The first was the transfer argument: that curriculum integration enables students to learn how to transfer knowledge and skills across contexts, in particular from one discipline to another, and to apply their knowledge and skills where and when they are needed. Second was the focus argument: that an integrated curriculum enables better learning because the students' attention is focused on a few, big, shared ideas or topics, rather than a multiplicity of different, unconnected ideas. Third was the motivation argument: that students, especially adolescent students, are more likely to be engaged when the curriculum is about things that are relevant to their world beyond the classroom, including their local community and/or issues and concerns important to their friends and family.

5. The Worldly Perspective acknowledges that learning contexts shape the nature of the enacted curriculum and that, in turn, shapes the nature of student learning

In Chapter 4, we explained how our research revealed the importance of the educational context to the implementation of integrated curricula and the resultant student learning. Factors that determine the educational context are as diverse as the expectations of parents, the nature of state and national assessment strategies, the background experience of individual teachers and the physical structure of the school classrooms, and those factors can and do impact on how an integrated curriculum is implemented. The Worldly Perspective acknowledges that similar goals for integrated curricula may result in different approaches and learning outcomes. Teachers and educational researchers are urged to examine how learning contexts shape the nature of the enacted curriculum, and how that, in turn, shapes the nature of students' learning.

6. The Worldly Perspective advocates the use of a variety of learning lenses, for example, a disciplinary lens, an integrated lens and a sources of knowledge lens

We found during our research that when we used different theoretical frameworks, or learning lenses, to make judgements about the teaching and learning that we observed, our conclusions about the observed outcomes changed. For example, an integrated learning lens compared with a disciplinary learning lens provided quite different, but complementary, images of students' learning. This phenomenon is described in a recent publication in the *Journal of Curriculum Studies* (Rennie *et al.*, 2011) and also in Chapter 4 of this book. What might be considered to be poor teaching and inadequate learning through a discipline-based learning lens, because students failed to learn a particular discipline-based concept, may be considered highly successful through an integrated learning lens because the students were able to apply what they had learnt to a real-world context. It became very clear to us that, when observing teaching and learning phenomena, the learning lenses used are critically important to the conclusions that will be reached. The Worldly Perspective advocates the use of a variety of lenses to evaluate student learning in integrated curriculum settings.

7. The Worldly Perspective advocates balance between disciplinary and integrated knowledge and connection between local and global knowledge

In Chapters 5 and 6 of this book we demonstrated the inadequacy of current frameworks used to judge the power of the knowledge promoted by particular approaches to curriculum. We questioned the authority of frameworks that bestow power on only the narrow, fragmented, isolated, theoretical, canonical knowledge developed as part of strongly discipline-based curricula. In our view, these frameworks failed to capture the power of the type of knowledge that is likely to be developed as a result of students participating in an integrated curriculum. In Chapter 6 we argued that integrated curricula are more appropriately analysed and judged through two dimensions. The first dimension, the knowledge dimension, can be used to indicate the degree of balance between disciplinary knowledge and integrated knowledge. The greater the balance between these types of knowledge, the more power the curriculum is likely to provide to the students engaged in that curriculum. The second dimension, the locality dimension, can be used to indicate the degree of connection between local types of knowledge and global types of knowledge considered though the curriculum: The greater the degree of connection between local and global knowledge, the greater the power of the curriculum for students in the global world of the twenty-first century.

Conclusion

We conclude by noting that the questions that we asked about curriculum were not very different to those asked by Tyler (1949) more than six decades ago, and discussed in Chapter 1. Tyler's first question remains fundamental: 'What educational purposes should the school seek to attain?' Our belief in writing this book was that schools should seek to provide students with the knowledge that prepares them to be responsible adults and sensible citizens in a rapidly changing global environment. In this volume we have explored the contribution that can be made by integrated curriculum. We concluded that varying approaches to curriculum integration abound, and their nature and outcomes are dependent on many factors. We endeavoured to understand and capture this variety using a Worldly Perspective which, to us, is the crux to understanding the two significant dimensions of curriculum – the balance between disciplinary knowledge and integrated knowledge, and the connection between local types of knowledge and global types of knowledge. We recognize that the point of balance and degree of connection are dependent on curriculum context; indeed, the Worldly Perspective demands that this be so. What we argue is that the best chance of providing our youth with knowledge that counts is to offer a curriculum that achieves both balance and connection and so provides students with powerful knowledge to negotiate and improve the global community in which they live.

Bibliography

Aikenhead, G. (2006). *Science education for everyday life. Evidence-based practice.* New York: Teachers College Press.

Alleman, J., and Brophy, J. (1993). Is curriculum integration a boon or a threat to social studies? *Social Education, 57*(6), 287–291.

Anderson, L. (1977). Global education: An overview. *Social Education, 41*(4), 35–36.

Apple, M. W., and Beane, J. A. (1999). Lessons from democratic schools. In M. W. Apple and J. A. Beane (Eds.), *Democratic schools: Lessons from the chalk face* (pp. 118–123). Buckingham, UK: Open University Press.

Applebee, A. N., Adler, M., and Flihan, S. (2007). Interdisciplinary curricula in middle and high school classrooms: Case studies of approaches to curriculum and instruction. *American Educational Research Journal, 44*(4), 1007–1039.

Au, W. (2007). High-stakes testing and curricular control: A qualitative metasynthesis. *Educational Researcher, 36*(5), 258–267.

Australian Curriculum Assessment and Reporting Authority (ACARA) (2010). *Australian Curriculum: Science.* Retrieved January 10, 2011, from http://www.australiancurriculum.edu.au/Science/Rationale.

Bakhtin, M. M. (1981). *The dialogic imagination: Four essays* (C. Emerson and M. Holdquist, Trans.). Austin, TX: University of Texas Press.

Ballantyne, R., Connell, S., and Fien, J. (2006). Students as catalysts of environmental change: A framework for researching intergenerational influence through environmental education. *Environmental Education Research, 12*(3–4), 413.

Beane, J. A. (1991). The middle school: The natural home of integrated curriculum. *Educational Leadership, 49*(2), 9–13.

Beane, J. A. (1995). Curriculum integration and the disciplines of knowledge. *Phi Delta Kappan, 76*(8), 616–622.

Beane, J. A. (1996). On the shoulders of giants! The case for curriculum integration. *Middle School Journal, 28*(1), 6–11.

Berlin, D. F., and Lee, H. (2005). Integrating science and mathematics education: Historical analysis. *School Science and Mathematics, 105*(1), 15–24.

Bernstein, B. (1971). On classification and framing of educational knowledge. In M. F. D. Young (Ed.), *Knowledge and control: New directions for the sociology of education* (pp. 47–69). London: Collier–Macmillan.

Bernstein, B. (2000). *Pedagogy, symbolic control and identity: Theory, research, critique* (rev. ed.). Lanham, MD: Rowman & Littlefield.

Bhabha, H. K. (1995). Cultural diversity and cultural differences. In B. Ashcroft, G. Griffiths and H. Tiffin (Eds.), *The post-colonial studies reader* (pp. 206–212). New York: Routledge.

Bianchini, J. A., and Kelly, G. J. (2003). Challenges of standards-based reform: The example of California's science content standards and textbook adoption process. *Science Education, 87*(3), 378–389.

Bouillion, L. M., and Gomez, L. M. (2001). Connecting school and community with science learning: Real world problems and school–community partnerships as contextual scaffolds. *Journal of Research in Science Teaching, 38*(8), 878–898.

Brantlinger, E., and Majd-Jabbari, M. (1998). The conflicted pedagogical and curricular perspectives of middle class mothers. *Journal of Curriculum Studies, 30*(4), 431–460.

Briggs, J., and Peat, F. D. (1999). *Seven life lessons of chaos: Timeless wisdom from the science of change.* New York: Harper Collins.

Brown, S. A. (1977). A review of the meanings of, and arguments for, integrated science. *Studies in Science Education, 4*, 31–62.

Bruner, J. S. (1960). *The process of education.* Cambridge, MA: Harvard University Press.

Buxton, C. A. (2006). Creating contextually authentic science in a 'low-performing' urban elementary school. *Journal of Research in Science Teaching, 43*(7), 695–721.

California Department of Education (1999). *Instructional materials in California: An overview of standards, curriculum frameworks, instructional materials adoptions, and funding.* Sacramento, CA: California Department of Education. Retrieved March 2, 2010, from www.cde.ca.gov/be/pn/im/documents/info-cib-cfir-jun06item01.doc.

Capra, F. (1982). *The turning point: Science, society and the rising culture.* New York: Simon & Schuster.

Capra, F. (1996). *The web of life: A new scientific understanding of living systems.* New York: Anchor Books.

Carr, D. (2007). Towards an educationally meaningful curriculum: Epistemic holism and knowledge integration revisited. *British Journal of Educational Studies, 55*(1), 3–20.

Carter, L. (2008). Globalization and science education: The implications of science in the new economy. *Journal of Research in Science Teaching, 45*(5), 617–633.

Case, R. (1994). Our crude handling of education reforms: The case of curricular integration. *Canadian Journal of Education, 19*(1), 80–93.

Case, R. (1997). Global education: It's largely a matter of perspective. In R. Case and P. Clarke (Eds.), *The Canadian anthology of social studies: Issues and strategies for teachers* (pp. 75–82). Burnaby, BC: Simon Fraser University.

Clark, E. T. Jr. (1997). *Designing and implementing an integrated curriculum.* Brandon, VT: Holistic Education Press.

Clement, J. (1987). Overcoming misconceptions in physics: The role of anchoring intuition and analogical validity. In J. Novak (Ed.), *Proceedings of the 2nd International Seminar on Misconceptions and Educational Strategies in Science and Mathematics, III* (pp. 84–97). Ithaca, NY: Cornell University.

Conservation gains a technical solution (2010, March 3). *The Australian Higher Education Supplement,* p. 24.

Coughlin, C. A., and Kirch, S. A. (2010). Place-based education: A transformative activist stance. *Cultural Studies of Science Education, 5*(4), 911–921.

Cumming, J. (1996). *From alienation to engagement: Opportunities for reform in the middle years of schooling* (Vol. 3). Canberra, Australia: Australian Curriculum Studies Association.

Curriculum Council of Western Australia. (1998). *Curriculum framework for kindergarten to Year 12 education in Western Australia*. Osborne Park, Western Australia: Author.

Czerniak, C. M. (2007). Interdisciplinary science teaching. In S. K. Abell and N. G. Lederman (Eds.), *Handbook of research on science education* (pp. 537–559). Mahwah, NJ: Lawrence Erlbaum Associates.

Czerniak, C. M., Weber, W. B., Sandmann, A., and Ahern, J. (1999). A literature review of science and mathematics integration. *School Science and Mathematics, 99*(8), 421–430.

Davis, B., Sumara, D., and Luce-Kapler, R. (2000). *Engaging minds: Learning and teaching in a complex world*. San Francisco: Jossey–Bass.

Davis, K. S. (2004, April). *Disrupting images of inability and failure: Middle school students as knowledge producers through project based instruction*. Paper presented at the annual meeting of the National Association for Research in Science Teaching, Vancouver, BC.

de Brabander, C. J. (2000). Knowledge definition, subject, and educational track level: Perceptions of secondary school teachers. *American Educational Research Journal, 37*(4), 1027–1058.

Deal, T. E., and Kennedy, A. A. (1982). *Corporate cultures*. Reading, MA: Addison Wesley.

Department for Employment and Education (2000). *The National Curriculum: Handbook for secondary teachers in England*. London: Author.

Department for Employment and Education (2011). *Review of the National Curriculum*. Retrieved January 22, 2011, from http://www.education.gov.uk/schools/teachingandlearning/curriculum/nationalcurriculum

Dewey, J. (1902). *The child and the curriculum*. Chicago: University of Chicago Press.

Dewey, J. (1915/1900). *The school and society* (rev. ed.). Chicago: University of Chicago Press.

Dewey, J. (1916). *Democracy and education*. New York: Macmillan.

Dillon, J. T. (2009). The questions of curriculum. *Journal of Curriculum Studies, 41*(3), 343–359.

Drake, S. M. (1993). *Planning integrated curriculum: The call to adventure*. Alexandria, VA: Association for Supervision and Curriculum Development.

Drake, S. M. (1998). *Creating integrated curriculum: Proven ways to increase student learning*. Thousand Oaks, CA: Corwin Press.

Duschl, R. (2008). Science education in three-part harmony: Balancing conceptual, epistemic, and social learning goals. In G. J. Kelly, A. Luke, and J. Green (Vol. Eds.), *Review of Educational Research: What counts as knowledge in educational settings* (Vol. 32, pp. 292–327). Thousand Oaks, CA: Sage.

Evans, R., Koul, R., and Rennie, L. (2007). Raising environmental awareness through a school–community partnership. *Teaching Science, 55*(1), 30–34.

Eyers, V. (1992). *The middle years of schooling: The education of young adolescents, years six to nine* (Seminar Series). Melbourne, Australia: Incorporated Association of Registered Teachers of Victoria.

Flowers, N., Mertens, S. B., and Mulhall, P. F. (2003). Middle school renewal: Lessons learned from more than a decade of middle grades research. *Middle School Journal, 35*(2), 55–59.

Fogarty, R. (1991). Ten ways to integrate the curriculum. *Educational Leadership, 49*(2), 61–65.

Fogarty, R. (2002). *How to integrate the curricula* (2nd ed.). Thousand Oaks, CA: Corwin Press.

Gardner, H. (2004). Discipline, understanding, and community. *Journal of Curriculum Studies, 36*(2), 233–236.

Gardner, H., and Boix-Mansilla, V. (1994). Teaching for understanding – within and across the disciplines. *Educational Leadership, 51*(5), 14–18.

Gardner, P. L. (1975). Science and the structure of knowledge. In P. L. Gardner (Ed.), *The structure of science education* (pp. 1–40). Hawthorne, Australia: Longman.

Gautier, C., Deutsch, K., and Rebich, S. (2006). Misconceptions about the greenhouse effect. *Journal of Geoscience Education, 54*(3), 386–396.

Gehrke, N. J. (1998). A look at curriculum integration from the bridge. *The Curriculum Journal, 9*(2), 247–260.

González, N. (2004). Disciplining the discipline: Anthropology and the pursuit of quality education. *Educational Researcher, 33*(5), 17–25.

Goodson, I. F. (1992). Studying school subjects. *Curriculum Perspectives, 12*(1), 23–26.

Gruenewald, D. A. (2003). The best of both worlds: A critical pedagogy of place. *Educational Researcher, 32*(4), 3–12.

Gruenewald, D. A. and Smith, G. A. (2008). Introduction: Making room for the local. In D. A. Gruenewald and G. A. Smith (Eds.), *Place-based education in the global age: Local diversity* (pp. xiii–xxiii). New York: Lawrence Erlbaum Associates.

Habermas, J. (1971). *Knowledge and human interests* (J. Shapiro, Trans.). Boston, MA: Beacon Press.

Haggis, S., and Adey, P. (1979). A review of integrated science education worldwide. *Studies in Science Education, 6*, 69–89.

Hall, C., and Kidman, J. (2004). Teaching and learning: Mapping the contextual influences. *International Education Journal, 5*(3), 331–343.

Hameyer, U. (2007). Transforming domain knowledge: A systemic view at the school curriculum. *The Curriculum Journal, 18*(4), 411–427.

Hargreaves, A., and Earl, L. (1990). *Rights of passage: A review of selected research about schooling in the transition years*. A report of a research project funded under contract by the Ministry of Education. Toronto, ON: Ontario Ministry of Education.

Hargreaves, A., and Moore, S. (2000). Curriculum integration and classroom relevance: A study of teachers' practice. *Journal of Curriculum and Supervision, 15*(2), 89–112.

Hargreaves, A., Earl, L., and Ryan, J. (1996). *Schooling for change: Reinventing education for early adolescents*. London: Falmer.

Hargreaves, A., Earl, L., Moore, S., and Manning, S. (2001). *Learning to change: Teaching beyond subjects and standards*. San Francisco, CA: Jossey–Bass.

Hatch, T. (1998). The differences in theory that matter in the practice of school improvement. *American Educational Research Journal, 35*(1), 3–31.

Hirst, P. H., and Peters, R. S. (1970). *The logic of education*. London: Routledge.

Hodson, D. (2003). Time for action: Science education for an alternative future. *International Journal of Science Education, 25*(6), 645–670.

Hurley, M. M. (2001). Reviewing integrated science and mathematics: The search for evidence and definitions from new perspectives. *School Science and Mathematics, 101*(5), 259–268.

Jacobs, H. (Ed.) (1989). *Interdisciplinary curriculum: Design and implementation*. Alexandria, VA: Association for Supervision and Curriculum Development.

Jenkins, E. (2007). School science: A questionable construct? *Journal of Curriculum Studies, 39*(3), 265–282.

Johnson, M. D. (2004). The newest 'reality show:' The importance of legitimizing experiential learning with community-based research. *The American Biology Teacher, 66*(8), 549–553.

Kain, D. L. (1996). Recipes or dialogue? A middle school team conceptualizes 'curricular integration.' *Journal of Curriculum and Supervision, 11*(2), 163–188.

Kaplan, L. S. (1997). Parents' rights: Are middle schools at risk? *Schools in the Middle, 7*(1), 35–38, 48.

Kelly, G. J., Luke, A., and Green, J. (Eds.) (2008). What counts as knowledge in educational settings: Disciplinary knowledge, assessment, and curriculum. *Review of Research in Education: What counts as knowledge in educational settings, disciplinary knowledge, assessment, and curriculum* (Vol. 32, pp. vii–x). Thousand Oaks, CA: Sage.

Kliebard, H. (1986). *The struggle for the American curriculum, 1893–1958.* Boston, MA: Routledge & Kegan Paul.

Kruse, R. A., and Roehrig, G. H. (2005). A comparison study: Assessing teachers' conceptions with the Chemistry Concepts Inventory. *Journal of Chemical Education, 82*(8), 1246–1250.

Kysilka, M. L. (1998). Understanding integrated curriculum. *The Curriculum Journal, 9*(2), 197–209.

Lederman, N. G., and Niess, M. L. (1998). 5 apples + 3 oranges +? *School Science and Mathematics, 98*(6), 281–284.

Lee, H-S., and Songer, N. B. (2003). Making authentic science accessible to students. *International Journal of Science Education, 25*(8), 923–948.

Leonardo, Z. (2004). Disciplinary knowledge and quality education (Editor's introduction to theme issue). *Educational Researcher, 33*(5), 3–5.

Levinson, R. (2001). Should controversial issues in science be taught through the humanities? *School Science Review, 82*(300), 97–101.

Lingard, B., Ladwig, L., Luke, A., Mills, M., Hayes, D., and Gore, J. (2001). *Queensland school reform longitudinal study: Final report.* Brisbane, Australia: Education Queensland:

Lloyd, D., and Wallace, J. (2004). Imagining the future of science education: The case for making futures studies explicit in student learning. *Studies in Science Education, 39*, 139–177.

Lyons, T., and Quinn, F. (2010). *Choosing science: Understanding the declines in senior high school science enrolments.* Armidale, NSW, Australia: National Centre of Science, ICT and Mathematics Education for Rural and Regional Australia (SiMERR Australia), University of New England. Retrieved February 15, 2010, from www.une.edu.au/ simerr.

MacMath, S., Wallace, J., and Chi, X. (2008a). *Curriculum integration project, Technical report #1, Rinkview.* Toronto, ON: Centre for Science, Mathematics and Technology Education, OISE, University of Toronto.

MacMath, S., Wallace, J., and Chi, X. (2008b). *Curriculum integration project, Technical report #2, Greenwich.* Toronto, ON: Centre for Science, Mathematics and Technology Education, OISE, University of Toronto.

MacMath, S., Wallace, J., and Chi, X. (2008c). *Curriculum integration project, Technical report #3, Beachville.* Toronto, ON: Centre for Science, Mathematics and Technology Education, OISE, University of Toronto.

MacMath, S., Wallace, J., and Chi, X. (2009). Curriculum integration: Opportunities to maximize assessment *as, of,* and *for* learning. *McGill Journal of Education, 44*(3), 451–465.

MacMath, S., Roberts, J., Wallace, J., and Chi, X. (2010). Curriculum integration and at risk students: A Canadian case study examining student learning and motivation. *British Journal of Special Education, 37*(2), 87–94.

Marsh, C. J. (1993, November). *How achievable is curriculum integration? Practices and issues.* Paper presented at the 10th Hong Kong Educational Research Association Conference, Hong Kong.

Meeth, R. L. (1978). Interdisciplinary studies: A matter of definition. *Change, 10*(7), 10.

Miller, J. (2007). *The holistic curriculum* (2nd ed.). Toronto, ON: University of Toronto Press.

Mundy, K., Manion, C., Masemann, V., and Haggerty, M. (2007). *Charting global education in Canada's elementary schools: Provincial, district and school level perspectives.* Toronto, ON: Ontario Institute of Science Education and UNICEF.

National Research Council. (1996). *National science education standards.* Washington, DC: National Academy Press.

Newman, R. S., and Schwager, M. T. (1992). Student perceptions and academic help-seeking. In D. H. Schunk and J. L. Meece (Eds.), *Student perceptions in the classroom* (pp. 123–146). Hillsdale, NJ: Lawrence Erlbaum.

O'Loughlin, M. (1994). Being and knowing: Self and knowledge in early adolescence. *Curriculum Perspectives, 14*(3), 44–46.

Osborne, J., Simon, S., and Collins, S. (2003). Attitudes towards science: A review of the literature and its implications. *International Journal of Science Education, 25*(9), 1049–1079.

Pang, J. S., and Good, R. (2000). A review of the integration of science and mathematics: Implications for further research. *School Science and Mathematics, 100*(2), 73–82.

Parker, L. (1994). *The gender code of school science* (Unpublished doctoral thesis). Curtin University of Technology, Perth, Western Australia.

Pedretti, E. (2005). STSE education: Principles and practices. In S. Alsop, L. Bencze and E. Pedretti (Eds.), *Analyzing exemplary science teaching: Theoretical lenses and a spectrum of possibilities for practice* (pp. 116–126). London: Open University Press.

Pendergast, D., Flanagan, R., Land, R., Bahr, M., Mitchell, J., Weir, K., et al. (2005). *Developing lifelong learners in the middle years of schooling.* Melbourne, Australia: Ministerial Council on Education, Employment and Youth Affairs.

Perkins, D. N., and Simmons, R. (1988). Patterns of misunderstanding: An integrative model for science, math, and programming. *Review of Educational Research, 58*(3), 303–326.

Ravetz, J. R. (2005). *The no nonsense guide to science.* Oxford, UK: New Internationalist Publications.

Reiss, M. J., and Tunnicliffe, S. D. (1999, March). *Building a model of the environment: How do children see plants?* Paper presented at the annual meeting of the National Association for Research in Science Teaching, Boston, MA.

Rennie, L. J. (2007). What counts as science education? *Studies in Science Education, 43,* 135–143.

Rennie, L. J., Venville, G., and Wallace, J. (2011). Learning science in an integrated classroom: Finding balance through theoretical triangulation. *Journal of Curriculum Studies, 43*(2), 139–162.

Ritchie, S. M., and Hampson, B. (1996). Learning in-the-making: A case study of science and technology projects in a Year 6 classroom. *Research in Science Education, 26*(4), 391–407.

Rivet, A. E., and Krajcik, J. S. (2008). Contextualizing instruction: Leveraging students' prior knowledge and experiences to foster understanding of middle school science. *Journal of Research in Science Teaching, 45*(1), 79–100.

Roderick, M., and Camburn, E. (1999). Risk and recovery from course failure in the early years of high school. *American Education Research Journal, 36*(2), 303–343.

Rogers, B. (1997). Informing the shape of the curriculum: New views of knowledge and its representation in schooling. *Journal of Curriculum Studies, 29*(6), 683–710.

Ross, J. A., and Hogaboam-Gray, A. (1998). Integrating mathematics, science, and technology: Effects on students. *International Journal of Science Education, 20*(9), 1119–1135.

Roth, W.-M. (1998). *Designing communities.* Dordrecht, The Netherlands: Kluwer.

Rowbotham, J. (2010, March 3). Researchers aim to build a case on bones. *The Australian Higher Education Supplement*, p. 21.

Schoenfeld, A. H. (2004). Multiple learning communities: Students, teachers, instructional designers, and researchers. *Journal of Curriculum Studies, 36*(2), 237–255.

Schwab, J. J. (1964). Structure of the disciplines: Meanings and significances. In G. W. Ford and L. Pugno (Eds.), *The structure of knowledge and the curriculum* (pp. 31–49). New York: Rand McNally.

Scott, D. (2008). *Critical essays on major curriculum theorists.* London: Routledge.

Sheffield, R., and Al-baghdadi, R. (2006). An integrated house project: Bringing together science with other learning areas. *Teaching Science, 52*(3), 37–41.

Sheffield, R., Venville, G., and Rennie, L. J. (2008, July). *Issues relating to shared leadership in a cross curricular science project.* Paper presented at the annual conference of the Australasian Science Education Research Association, Brisbane, Australia.

Shulman, L. S., and Sherin, M. (2004). Fostering communities of teachers as learners: Disciplinary perspectives. *Journal of Curriculum Studies, 36*(2), 135–140.

Sirotnik, K. (1983). What you see is what you get: Consistency, persistency and mediocrity in classrooms. *Harvard Education Review, 53*(1), 16–31.

Siskin, L. S. (1994). *Realms of knowledge: Academic departments in secondary schools.* London: Falmer.

Smith, D. L., and Lovat, T. J. (2003). *Curriculum: Action on reflection* (4th ed.). Tuggerah, NSW, Australia: Social Science Press.

Stengel, B. S. (1997). 'Academic discipline' and 'school subject': Contestable curricular concepts. *Journal of Curriculum Studies, 29*(5), 585–602.

Thomson, S., and De Bortoli, L. (2008). *Exploring scientific literacy: How Australia measures up. The PISA 2006 survey of students' scientific, reading and mathematical literacy skills.* Camberwell, Victoria, Australia: ACER Press.

Tirosh, D., and Stavy, R. (1992). Students' ability to confine their application of knowledge: The case of mathematics and science. *School Science and Mathematics, 92*(7), 353–358.

Trounson, A. (2010, February 24). Deep specialization key to collaboration. *The Australian Higher Education Supplement*, p. 23.

Tylack, D., and Tobin, W. (1994). The grammar of schooling: Why has it been so hard to change? *American Educational Research Journal, 31*(3), 453–480.

Tyler, R. W. (1949). *Basic principles of curriculum and instruction*. Chicago: University of Chicago Press.

Van Eijck, M., and Roth, W.-M. (2010). Towards a chronotopic theory of 'place' in place-based education. *Cultural Studies of Science Education, 5*(4), 869–898.

Vars, G. F. (1991). Integrated curriculum in historical perspective. *Educational Leadership, 49*(2), 14–15.

Venville, G., Wallace, J., Rennie, L., and Malone, J. (1999a). *Science, mathematics and technology case studies of integrated teaching*. Perth, Australia: Curtin University of Technology and Education Department of Western Australia, Perth.

Venville, G., Wallace, J., Rennie, L., and Malone, J. (1999b). Building bridges across the disciplines: Learning science through technology. *The Journal of Design and Technology Education, 4*(1), 40–45.

Venville, G., Wallace, J., Rennie, L., and Malone, J. (2000). Bridging the boundaries of compartmentalized knowledge: Student learning in an integrated environment. *Research in Science and Technological Education, 18*(1), 23–35.

Venville, G., Wallace, J., Rennie, L., and Malone, J. (2002). Curriculum integration: Eroding the high ground of science as a school subject? *Studies in Science Education, 37*, 43–84.

Venville, G., Rennie, L., and Wallace, J. (2003). Student understanding and application of science concepts in the context of an integrated curriculum setting. *International Journal of Science and Mathematics Education, 1*(4), 449–475.

Venville, G., Rennie, L., and Wallace, J. (2004). Decision making and sources of knowledge: How students tackle integrated tasks in science, technology and mathematics. *Research in Science Education, 34*(2), 115–135.

Venville, G., Sheffield, R., Rennie, L. J., and Wallace, J. (2008). The writing on the wall: Classroom context, curriculum implementation, and student learning in integrated, community-based projects. *Journal of Research in Science Teaching, 45*(8), 857–880.

Venville, G., Rennie, L., and Wallace, J. (in press). Curriculum integration: Challenging the assumption of school science as powerful knowledge. In B. Fraser, K. Tobin and C. McRobbie (Eds.), *International handbook of research in science education* (2nd ed.). Dordrecht, The Netherlands: Springer.

Viennot, L., and Rozier, S. (1994). Pedagogical outcomes of research in science education: Examples in mechanics and thermodynamics. In P. J. Fensham, R. F. Gunstone and R. T. White (Eds.), *The content of science: A constructivist approach to its teaching and learning* (pp. 237–254). London: Falmer Press.

Visher, M. G., Emanuel, D., and Teitelbaum, P. (1999). *Key high school reform strategies: An overview of research findings*. Berkeley, CA: MPR Associates.

Wallace, J., Rennie, L., Malone, J., and Venville, G. (2001). What we know and what we need to know about curriculum integration in science, mathematics and technology. *Curriculum Perspectives, 21*(1), 9–15.

Wallace, J., Sheffield, R., Rennie, L., and Venville, G. (2007). Looking back, looking forward: Re-searching the conditions for integration in the middle years of schooling. *Australian Educational Researcher, 34*(2), 29–49.

Wilson, E. O. (1998). *Consilience: The unity of knowledge*. New York: Vintage.

Wood, N. B., Lawrenz, F., Huffman, D., and Schultz, M. (2006). Viewing the school environment through multiple lenses: In search of school-level variables tied to student achievement. *Journal of Research in Science Teaching, 43*(3), 237–254.

Young, D., and Gehrke, N. (1993). Curriculum integration for transcendence: A critical review of recent books on curriculum integration. *Curriculum Inquiry, 23*(4), 445–454.

Young, M. (2008). From constructivism to realism in the sociology of the curriculum. In G. J. Kelly, A. Luke and J. Green (Vol. Eds.), *Review of Research in Education: What counts as knowledge in educational setting* (Vol. 32, pp. 1–28). Thousand Oaks, CA: Sage.

Appendix   Description of case studies of integrated curriculum

Pseudonym school name	Description of school	Nature of data collected	Integration practice during study	Report of case study
Beachville Secondary School	Large suburban secondary school, Years 9 to 12	Classroom observations, pre-, during and post- interviews with 7 students, post survey of whole class, interviews with 2 teachers	*Synchronized approach*: For a Year 9 applied class, the geography and science teachers collaborated to teach the 5-week energy topic separately but in parallel. In geography and in science, cross-curricular links and concepts were reinforced	MacMath, Wallace and Chi (2008c) MacMath, Roberts, Wallace and Chi (2010)
Brampton High School	Large urban secondary school, Years 8 to 12	Classroom observations, student surveys, interviews with 1 teacher and science coordinator and groups of students, documentary analysis	*Community-focused approach*: A Year 9 academic extension class had their 10-week ecology topic in science expanded to include a study of midge (small water breeding insects) in the local wetland and their effects on the community	Venville *et al.* (2008)

Continued

Pseudonym school name	Description of school	Nature of data collected	Integration practice during study	Report of case study
Chelsea Primary School	Small, independent primary school in urban area, Years K to 7	Classroom observations, student surveys, interviews with 2 teachers, the programme coordinator, wildlife centre manager, groups of students, documentary analysis	*Community-focused approach*: Two combined Year 4 to 7 classes worked closely with a wildlife centre on an integrated programme aimed at understanding, and living with, tiger snakes. All school subjects were involved and the 8-week long focus culminated in a community presentation by students	Evans, Koul and Rennie (2007)
Eagleton Senior High School	Large urban secondary school, Years 8 to 10	Extensive interviews with 3 teachers, classroom observations over one term, detailed interviews with 6 students, documentary analysis	*Project-based approach*: The science, mathematics and technology teachers worked as a team to teach the Years 8–10 academic extension programme through integrated technology-based projects (e.g., design and building of a solar powered boat)	Venville *et al.* (1999a) Venville *et al.* (2000) Venville *et al.* (2003) Venville *et al.* (2004) Rennie *et al.* (2011)
Florabunda District High School	Middle-size regional school in mining community, Years K to 10, high Indigenous population	School visit for 2 days, detailed interviews with 2 teachers, informal interviews with the principal and 4 other teachers, documentary analysis	*Thematic approach*: The curriculum in Years 8, 9 and 10 was organized around term themes (e.g. relationships, the Olympics), incorporating aspects from each learning area	Venville *et al.* (1999a)

Continued

Pseudonym school name	Description of school	Nature of data collected	Integration practice during study	Report of case study
Gosport Community School	Large suburban middle school, Years 6 to 9	Classroom observations, student surveys, interviews with 1 teacher, area coordinator and groups of students, documentary analysis	*Thematic approach*: Two Year 8 classes engaged in a 10-week module about community access for disabled people. Disability was considered in science, social studies, health and other subject areas	Sheffield, Venville and Rennie (2008)
Greenbelt Community College	New, large, urban middle school, Years 7 to 9	School visits, interviews with 7 teachers, 2 deputy principals and the principal, documentary analysis	*Thematic approach*: The Year 7, 8 and 9 teachers worked collaboratively in learning teams to design, implement and assess interdisciplinary modules (e.g., my heritage, patterns in life) leading to disciplinary and interdisciplinary outcomes	Venville *et al.* (1999a)
Greenwich Public School	Middle-sized suburban primary school, Years K to 6	Classroom observations, pre-, during and post-interviews with 10 students, post survey of whole class, interviews with the teacher	*Project-based approach*: One teacher and her Year 6 class worked on a 5-week integrated unit on the theme of ice hockey. Students were expected to select players for a fictional team, develop a game schedule and build an ice hockey rink to scale	MacMath *et al.* (2008b) MacMath *et al.* (2009)

Continued

Pseudonym school name	Description of school	Nature of data collected	Integration practice during study	Report of case study
Hedgerow Primary School	Large urban primary school, Years K to 7	School visit, interviews with 1 teacher, documentary analysis	*Cross-curricular approach*: Technology was an integrating subject across the curriculum, with students' design-and-make projects linked into other subject areas such as social studies, art and science, and the enterprise aspect linked to other subjects such as mathematics and literacy	Venville *et al.* (1999a)
Hillsdale Christian School	Small private suburban secondary school, Years 8 to 12	School visit, interviews with 2 teachers and principal, documentary analysis	*Community-focused approach*: The middle school mathematics and social studies teachers initiated a joint community-based project in their Year 10 class on the world's North–South inequities	Venville *et al.* (1999a)
Kentish Middle School	Large suburban middle school, Years 6 to 9	Classroom observations, student surveys, interviews with 2 teachers and groups of students, documentary analysis	*Community-focused approach*: A learning community of 120 Years 6 and 7 students undertook a 10-week, extensive study of the local wetland with an integrated approach involving water quality, land use, ecological studies, recycling and economic factors	Venville *et al.* (2008)

Continued

Pseudonym school name	Description of school	Nature of data collected	Integration practice during study	Report of case study
Mossburn School	Small, independent secondary school in suburban area, Years 8 to 12	Classroom observations, student surveys, interviews with 6 teachers, the project coordinator and groups of students, documentary analysis	*Project-based approach*: the Year 8 academic extension class built a model house and most subjects were involved. Teachers taught their own subject area but all taught sections of the 10-week-long project related to the design and building of the model house	Sheffield and Al-baghdadi (2006)
Oceanside Senior High School	Large urban secondary school, Years 8 to 12	School visits, interviews with 2 teachers, documentary analysis	*School-specialized approach*: This coastal high school developed a marine studies specialization. Each of the 'core' subject areas taught one specified unit of marine studies in each of Years 8, 9 and 10	Venville *et al.* (1999a)
Redwood High School	Large urban secondary school, Years 8 to 12	School visit, interviews with one teacher, documentary analysis	*Synchronized approach*: In the Year 8–10 academic extension programme, the science and mathematics teachers identified areas of curriculum overlap and taught integrated investigations twice a term	Venville *et al.* (1999a)

Continued

Pseudonym school name	Description of school	Nature of data collected	Integration practice during study	Report of case study
Rinkview Public School	Middle-sized suburban middle school, Years 6 to 8	Classroom observations, pre-, during and post-interviews with 12 students, post survey of whole class, interviews with 2 teachers	*Project-based approach*: Two Year 8 teachers joined classes to form a pod of 50 students to jointly teach a 6-week project-based unit on Making and Marketing a Toy. The students surveyed peers about possible toys, and designed, built and marketed their toy to other students	MacMath *et al.* (2008a) MacMath *et al.* (2009)
Riverview Ladies College	Large urban private girls' school, Years K to 12	School visits, interviews with 5 teachers, documentary analysis	*Thematic approach*: The five Year 8 teachers worked as a team to run integrated projects (e.g., environmental theme day) incorporating aspects of all learning areas	Venville *et al.* (1999a)
Sandbanks Community High School	Middle-sized new urban school, Years 8 to 9	School visits, interviews with 3 teachers, 2 deputy principals and principal, documentary analysis	*Thematic approach*: Teachers and students were organized into learning communities, with each community selecting and studying its own cross-curricular theme (e.g., decision making, environment) each term	Venville *et al.* (1999a)

Continued

Pseudonym school name	*Description of school*	*Nature of data collected*	*Integration practice during study*	*Report of case study*
Seaview Community School	Small, geographically isolated school, Years 1 to 10, students of Indigenous origin	Researcher resident at school for one week, interviews with all 3 teachers and principal, observations of Year 4 to 7 and Year 8 to 10 classrooms and outside activities, documentary analysis	*Cross-curricular approach:* A school-wide literary focus aimed at assisting students to learn English, which underpinned all subject areas and was supported by cross-curricular initiatives, such as horticulture relating to the school garden	Venville *et al.* (1999a)
Southern High School	Large urban secondary school, Years 8 to 12	Classroom observations of 7 of 10 lessons over five weeks, interviews with 1 teacher and 5 students, documentary analysis	*Project-based approach:* The Year 9 technology class was set a bridge-building project which incorporated knowledge of science, mathematics, engineering, design and construction. The aesthetics of the bridge were judged by the English teacher	Venville *et al.* (1999b)
Teatree Primary School	Large urban primary school, Years K to 7	School visit, interviews with Year 7 teacher and deputy principal, documentary analysis	*Thematic approach:* the Year 7 class raised chickens in a term-long project. School subjects, such as science, mathematics and technology were integral to the programme with other subjects, such as language, incorporated when appropriate	Venville *et al.* (1999a)

Author index

Adey, P. 2, 5
Adler, M. 19
Ahern, J. 61
Aikenhead, G. 14
Al-baghdadi, R. 134
Alleman, J. ix
Anderson, L. 101
Apple, M. W. 19
Applebee, A. N. 19, 49, 54–5
Au, W. 98
Australian Curriculum Assessment and Reporting Authority (ACARA) 77

Bahr, M. 45
Bakhtin, M. M. 100
Ballantyne, R. 102
Beane, J. A. ix, 6, 13, 19, 46, 55, 77, 92, 100
Berlin, D. F. 1
Bernstein, B. 35, 89, 90–3, 95–6, 99, 107, 114
Bhabha, H. K. 72
Bianchini, J. A. 78
Boix-Mansilla, V. 100
Bouillion, L. M. 19
Brabander, C. J. de 90–2, 94
Brantlinger, E. 36
Briggs, J. 75
Brophy, J. ix
Brown, S. A. 5
Bruner, J. S. 5, 74
Buxton, C. A. 19

California Department of Education 78
Camburn, E. 78

Capra, F. 75, 85
Carr, D. 3
Carter, L. 75
Case, R. ix, 101
Chi, X. 62, 130, 132
Clark, E. T. Jr. 14–7, 55
Clement, J. 83
Collins, S. 102
Connell, S. 102
Coughlin, C. A. 102–3
Cumming J. 65, 102
Curriculum Council of Western Australia 7, 92
Czerniak, C. M. 54, 61

Davis, B. 46
Davis, K. S. 56
De Bortoli, L. 102
Deal, T. E. 35
Department for Employment and Education 78
Deutsch, K. 102
Dewey, J. 5
Dillon, J. T. 3
Drake, S. M. ix, 12, 16, 18–9, 49, 55
Duschl, R. 96

Earl, L. 19, 77
Eijck, M. van 101–3
Emanuel, D. 45
Evans, R. 131
Eyers, V. 7

Fien, J. 102
Flanagan, R. 45
Flihan, S. 19

Flowers, N. 45
Fogarty, R. ix, 19, 49, 55, 100

Gardner, H. 76, 98, 100
Gardner, P. L. 74, 79
Gautier, C. 102
Gehrke, N. 1, 55, 77
Gomez, L. M. 19
González, N. 100
Good, R. 36, 67
Goodson, I. F. 77–8, 99
Gore, J. 37
Green, J. 14
Gruenewald, D. A. 19, 102–3

Habermas, J. 46, 85, 118
Haggerty, M. 101
Haggis, S. 2, 5
Hall, C. 35, 37
Hameyer, U. 74
Hampson, B. 69
Hargreaves, A. 19, 35, 45, 56, 65, 67,
    70, 77
Hatch, T. 13, 55, 77
Hayes, D. 37
Hirst, P. H. 106
Hodson, D. 85
Hogaboam-Gray, A. 56, 61–3, 65
Huffman, D. 35
Hurley, M. M. 54, 56

Jacobs, H. ix, 12, 17–20
Jenkins, E. 5, 75
Johnson, M. D. 85

Kain, D. L. 36
Kaplan, L. S. 37
Kelly, G. J. 14, 78, 96, 98
Kennedy, A. A. 35
Kidman, J. 35, 37
Kirch, S. A. 102–3
Kliebard, H. 78
Koul, R. 131
Krajcik, J. S. 19
Kruse, R. A. 36
Kysilka, M. L. 1, 18

Ladwig, L. 37
Land, R. 45

Lawrenz, F. 35
Lederman, N. G. 64
Lee, H. 1
Lee, H-S. 19
Leonardo, Z. 76–7, 100
Levinson, R. 36
Lingard, B. 37
Lloyd, D. 19, 46, 48–50
Lovat, T. J. 2
Luce-Kapler, R. 46
Luke, A. 14, 37
Lyons, T. 76

MacMath, S. 62, 103, 132, 135
Majd-Jabbari, M. 36
Malone, J. 9, 36
Manion, C. 101
Manning, S. 45, 56
Marsh, C. J. 19, 54
Masemann, V. 101
Meeth, R. L. 17–18, 20
Mertens, S. B. 45
Miller, J. 19
Mills, M. 37
Mitchell, J. 45
Moore, S. 45, 65
Mulhall, P. F. 45
Mundy, K. 101

National Research Council 78
Newman, R. S. 60
Niess, M. L. 64

O'Loughlin, M. 77
Osborne, J. 102

Pang, J. S. 36, 67
Parker, L. 90, 95
Peat, F. D. 75
Pedretti, E. 19
Pendergast, D. 45
Perkins, D. N. 56
Peters, R. S. 106

Quinn, F. 76

Ravetz, J. R. 85
Rebich, S. 102
Reiss, M. J. 60

Rennie, L. J. 9–11, 19, 36, 59, 90, 100, 119, 131–2
Ritchie, S. M. 69
Rivet, A. E. 19
Roberts, J. 103
Roderick, M. 78
Roehrig, G. H. 36
Rogers, B. 55, 57, 74–5, 78–80, 91
Ross, J. A. 56, 61–3, 65
Roth, W-M. 58, 60, 101–3
Rowbotham, J. 105–6
Rozier, S. 84
Ryan, J. 19, 35, 67, 70

Sandmann, A. 61
Schoenfeld, A. H. 76, 100
Schultz, M. 35
Schwab, J. J. 74
Schwager, M. T. 60
Scott, D. 3–4
Sheffield, R. 10, 132, 134
Sherin, M. 47
Shulman, L. S. 47
Simmons, R. 56
Simon, S. 102
Sirotnik, K. 65
Siskin, L. S. 78
Smith, D. L. 2
Smith, G. A. 19, 102–3

Songer, N. B. 19
Stavy, R. 64
Stengel, B. S. 74
Sumara, D. 46

Teitelbaum, P. 45
Thomson, S. 102
Tirosh, D. 64
Tobin, W. 11–2, 35, 106
Trounson, A. 76–7
Tunnicliffe, S. D. 60
Tylack, D. 11–2, 35, 106
Tyler, R. W. 3, 5, 120

Vars, G. F. 54
Venville, G. 9–11, 19, 36, 40–3, 45–8, 50, 58–9, 67, 82, 86, 99, 107–8, 116, 130–6
Viennot, L. 84
Visher, M. G. 45

Wallace, J. 9–13, 19, 36, 46, 48–50, 59, 62, 85, 103, 132
Weber, W. B. 61
Weir, K. 45
Wilson, E. O. 49
Wood, N. B. 35

Young, D. 55, 77
Young, M. 75–6, 95–6, 98–9, 107, 114

Subject index

approaches to integration 20–34, 117; community-focused 22, 31–3, 46, 52, 67–71, 85–9; cross-curricular 22, 27–9, 52; project-based 22, 25–7, 52, 67, 79–85, 117; school-specialized 22, 29–31, 52; synchronized 21–3, 117; thematic, 22–5, 52, 117

arguments: knowledge 73, 76–7; learning 57, 61, 118; focus 61, 63–5, 67, 71; motivation 61, 65–7; transfer 61–3, 67

assessment 4, 13, 56; achievement tests 54, 68, 98, 107; authentic 56, 71–2; portfolio of work 23; see also integrated curriculum, assessment in

case study schools 7–11; Beachville Secondary School 21–2, 38, 40, 42; Brampton High School 36, 44, 67–9, 71, 107–114; Chelsea Primary School 22, 31–3, 131; Eagleton Senior High School 22, 26–7, 38–9, 42, 44, 57–61, 71, 131; Florabunda District High School 38, 42–4, 131; Gosport Community School 132; Greenbelt Community College 22, 24–5, 38, 40–4, 132; Greenwich Public School 38, 62–6, 71, 132; Hedgerow Primary School 22, 27–8, 133; Hillsdale Christian School 38, 41, 44, 133; Kentish Middle School 22, 31, 36, 40–1, 44, 67–9, 71, 79, 85–9, 91–5, 133; Mossburn School 38, 41, 44, 134; Oceanside Senior High School 22, 30–1, 38, 41, 134; Redwood High School, 21–3, 38, 41, 44, 134;

Rinkview Public School 38, 40, 44, 62–6, 71, 135; Riverview Ladies College 22, 24, 38, 40, 43, 44, 135; Sandbanks Community High School 39, 40–1, 43–4, 135; Seaview Community School 22, 28–9, 39, 41, 44–5, 136; Southern High School 22, 26, 79–85, 91–5, 136; Teatree Primary School 136

community: global viii, 120; links 25, 28, 31–3, 44–5, 51, 71, 101–3; support 38–9, 53

connectedness 3, 15–7; between subjects 23, 25; with community 17, 30–1, 85, 95–6

connected world vii, 13, 53, 85, 95, 97, 101–3

continuum of integration 18–9, 34, 49, 55, 100, 103, 116

cross-disciplinary 17, 56, 61, 76–7

curriculum: balance in 14–5, 51, 114, 118; big ideas of 46, 49, 52, 64, 71; critical interest 48–9, 51–2, 85; dimensions of 3; discipline-based 4–6, 18, 33, 49, 53, 76–9, 98, 100–1, 112–3, 116; global 75; integration of 5–6, 12–3, 116–20, see also integrated curriculum; interests 37, 46, 99, 118; learner-centred 4, 6, 15–6, 55; meaning of 2; organization of 3–6, 20, 55, 74; practical interest 47–8, 51–2; purpose of viii, 3, 120; structure 5, 33–4, 46–9, 77–9, 85, 91, 106; subject-centred 4, 106; teacher-centred 4; technical interest 46–8, 51–2; Worldly Perspective on, see Worldly Perspective

decision-making 4
dimension: knowledge 97, 100–1, 103–7, 111–3; locality 97, 101–7, 113–5; multiple 19, 57

education: global 101; place-based 101–3; for citizenship 85; environmental 31–3, 102

grammar of schooling 11–2, 35, 106

help-seeking strategies 60–1

integrated curriculum: approaches to *see* approaches to integration; assessment in 14, 56, 71, 88–9, 93–4; attributes of 39–45; barriers to 12, 112; definition of 1, 19, 55, 70; enablers for 37–45, 117; implementation of 12, 35–53; inhibitors of 38–9, 117; meaning of viii-x, 1, 77; measurement in 56, 71; outcomes of 23, 25, 27, 29–31, 33, 54, 61, 69–70, 86–9, 100–1, 109–11; popularity of viii, 1, 6
interdisciplinary curriculum 12, 17–8, 20, 26, 34, 54–5
interests *see* curriculum interests

knowledge: bridged 58; balance between disciplinary and integrated 49, 51, 97, 100–1, 105–6, 114, 119–20; connections between local and global 14, 53, 96–7, 100–3, 105–6, 113–4, 119–20; disciplinary 34, 56–61, 67, 74, 79, 99, 117; holistic view of 36, 56, 75, 77, 106; integrated 34, 57; powerful 3, 89, 91, 95, 98–9, 114–5, 119; pedagogical 36, 53; profession-based 79–80; status of 13, 73–96, 98–9; structure of 73–9, 99; that counts viii, x, 14, 73, 95, 97–115, 120

leadership 38–42, 45
learner, needs of 2, 17, 18, 20, 49, 51, 75
learning 16; conceptual 59, 61, 68–70; contexts 57, 61, 67–72, 118–9; environment 39–40, 45; in integrated curriculum 13, 54–72, 83–9, 91–5, 99, 119; meaning-making as 16–7

lenses on learning 57–61, 71–2, 119; integrated lens 57–8, 60–1, 69; disciplinary lens 57, 59–61, 69; sources-of-knowledge lens 57, 59–61, 69
literacy: functional 14, 16; language 28–9; scientific 67, 86

middle-school viii, 7–9, 24, 31, 46, 56
multidisciplinary curriculum 12, 17–8, 20–1, 23, 25, 31, 34, 55, 112

parents 36–7, 44, 90, 98
perspective, Worldly *see* Worldly Perspective
place-based education *see* education, place-based
problem solving 18, 47–8, 51, 57–9, 64, 67, 71–2, 83, 93

research: methods 7–11, 62, 81–2, 86; programme 8

school: administrative support 38–9; case study, *see* case study schools; context 35–7, 112, 117; culture of, *see* grammar of schooling; disaffection with schooling vii-viii, 76; grammar of *see* grammar of schooling; resilient 51; social role of viii, 76, 98, 102; structure of 35, 37–45, 51, 68, 71, 77; timetable 28–9, 43–4, 68, 71–2, 108
subjects: boundaries between 18–9, 26, 28, 31, 33, 55, 89–95, 100, classification and frame of 35, 89–95; separate 58

teaching: commitment to 38–9; out of field 36, 38–9; planning time 38–9, 42–3, 45, 53, 68; teams 38–40, 42, 45; workload 38–9
transdisciplinary curriculum 12, 18, 20, 29, 31, 33–4, 55

values 32, 68–9, 92, 95, 99, 101

Worldly Perspective x, 12, 14, 37, 49–53, 56–7, 61, 70, 72, 97, 99–100, 104–7, 111–120